A NOBODY FOR EVERYBODY IN 2016

MY FINANCIAL FREEDOM PLAN FOR AMERICA

*Why Run a 21st Century Economy
On a 19th Century Operating System?*

Scott Smith

Illustrations by Steve Hussey
Cover Design by Thomas DeHart
Cover Photo of Candidate by Layla Smith

Self-Published
ISBN 978-1508649977
Paperback Black & White Edition

www.scottsmith2016.com

TABLE OF CONTENTS

CHAPTER ONE

A NOBODY FOR EVERYBODY
Four Solutions That Would Improve Your Life

*"Too often we enjoy the comfort of opinion without the
discomfort of thought."*
–John F. Kennedy

I HAVE COMMITTED to run for President with two
primary goals: to heal our economic wounds, and to end
the partisan warfare destroying our nation. My platform
appeals to both conservatives and liberals—a sharp
contrast to today's politics, which stirs up bitterness and
contempt, dividing the people of our nation and blinding
us to reality. The truth is, our current system undermines
both rich and poor. The solutions I propose provide a
better life for all.

Politically speaking, I am nobody. In reality I am a
revolutionary. In this book, I will present surprisingly
simple solutions to problems that previously seemed
insurmountable. You will find my approach to be
radically different from the partisan politics currently
destroying our nation. Mine is the approach of a political
outsider, independent of special interest groups, and

with a fresh perspective on the issues plaguing our nation.

Do I really think I can win? I do. The way I see it, voters want someone new. They want someone with real solutions—solutions they *know* will deliver a tangible and positive impact on their lives.

My wife and I had dinner recently with a couple and their 17-year old daughter. She started to check out when the conversation turned to economics, but then something caught her attention. My solutions actually made sense to her: she could see herself with more money in her pocket once she entered the workforce. Suddenly alert, she chimed in, "Wait a minute! Why aren't we doing this? I mean, we really should do this, right?"

Another evening I was in a cab in New Orleans, heading to the airport. The driver was cynical, as the last recession had hit him hard. I tried the solutions in this book on him, and his attitude began to change. Soon he was excited and fully engaged in our conversation. "Will they let you run?" he asked. "Isn't the whole thing rigged?"

When he let me out at the airport, he came around the cab to shake my hand. "I really do hope you run, sir," he said. "I understand what you say. I would have hope with this plan. People would like it."

THE MATERIAL VERSUS THE MONETARY ECONOMY

The reason for our current economic problems is simple: we are trying to run our 21st century economy on a 19th century operating system. We need to upgrade. Our current system is burdened with overhead that is no longer necessary.

The core concept behind my solutions is that there are really *two economies* at play in our world—the "material economy" and the "monetary economy." The material economy is the production and consumption of goods and services in the physical world: cars, planes, food, clothes, houses, haircuts, movies, and Disney rides. The monetary economy, on the other hand, is the synthetic world we have created: currency, stocks, bonds, mortgages, mutual funds, derivatives, interest, and dividends.

The most important aspect to remember is that *the monetary economy exists only to facilitate transactions in the material economy.* I expand on this in the seventh chapter, entitled "Down-Home Economics."

Many of our nation's challenges today stem from the fact that while technology has increased the efficiency of our material economy, there remain artificial barriers in the monetary system. These barriers produce scarcity instead of facilitating the abundance that our material economy could deliver. While the production engine in our material economy has grown stronger, able to deliver more for less,[1] our monetary economy is on a rollercoaster, periodically crashing and costing us jobs, bankrupting businesses, and destroying our wealth.[2]

That is why we need to upgrade: we are limited in our ability to improve the material economy if our monetary economy is working against us. This book presents upgrades to the financial system that would substantially increase your disposable income by slashing taxes and the cost of credit. For a family of four with a combined income of $100k, for example, the tax savings would be over $22k. For a homeowner with a $400k mortgage, the savings on mortgage payments would be $12k per year.

---

[1] It used to require a large portion of our population to grow the food we need, and today, because of technology, a much smaller portion of our population is able to produce a surplus of food.

[2] It is the artificial nature of the rollercoaster ride that is so tragic. While the producers and consumers in the material economy would like to produce and consume goods during a recession, they are unable to because of a crisis in the monetary system that stands in the way, often a liquidity or credit crisis.

In short, the disposable income of the average American family would nearly double under my plan, yet the national budget would not suffer. We would not need to cut federal spending, nor would we have a deficit.

Being a political nobody, my initial challenge will be fighting the charge that I am a nut. These are bold solutions, and there are professional politicians who will want to discredit me. I have faced this challenge before, and won. I was branded a heretic when I first proposed a structure for pooling mortgages on Wall Street, a story I describe in more detail in the final chapter of this book, entitled "My Journey." When the structure worked and Wall Street made billions, I was no longer a heretic. Math speaks for itself, and the truth has a way of winning out.

Years later, when Wall Street substituted credit default swaps for sound lending practices, the math spoke for itself again—this time in the form of a crash that devastated the lives of millions. The solutions in my platform are designed to protect us from such financial disasters. My platform instigates changes to the monetary economy that will improve our lives in the material economy.

A Better Operating System

Our financial system will never be perfect, as even the best system will have challenges and overhead. However, we can greatly improve our financial wellbeing by eliminating artificial barriers in our monetary economy that needlessly deplete our resources. The math works in the solutions I propose. The math does not work the way we are running our nation today.

Partisan politics come at the expense of one party or another; the solutions herein advance the wellbeing of everyone. The truth is, we *all* walk challenging paths, and we *all* suffer setbacks. And there is an even greater truth: *we are more economically interdependent than we think.*

The idea that improving our financial wellbeing can be synergistic—that is, that *each* of us can do better when we *all* do better—may seem radical, as we are accustomed to schemes in which one party succeeds at the expense of another. But it is time for such thinking to change.

Instead of pitting ourselves against each other, we need to focus on the root of the problem. It is because of our antiquated operating system that we have periodic recessions, which cause our nation's production engine to stumble. It is because of our antiquated operating system that we have chronic budget deficits, which result in skyrocketing debt. And because our operating system becomes increasingly outdated as time passes, the quality of our lives suffers more with each year that goes by. Some even project that today's young people will be the first generation financially worse off than their parents.[3]

The frustration we feel over these problems has led many to feel contempt for our leadership and despair for the future. The truth is that we are blessed with a production engine so robust it has withstood the headwinds imposed on it by our flawed tax and banking

3   http://www.businessinsider.com/younger-generations-are-worse-off-today-urban-institute-study-2013-3

systems for decades. A weaker engine would have failed long ago.

We have the most innovative, productive, and hardworking society in history. We are simply in need of a better financial operating system. The solutions in this book provide an elegant new operating system for our nation, reducing friction throughout the economy.

THE DAWNING OF A NEW AMERICAN DREAM

If we implement the solutions I propose, we will usher in a new era of wealth and prosperity. Your personal finances will dramatically improve, regardless of your income bracket. We will experience the dawning of a New American Dream.

My position on taxation is radical. Not even the most conservative candidate can come close to matching it, and yet, remarkably, it is also music to the ears of liberals; I am calling for a new operating system that allows each of us to keep all of our hard-earned income, without having to cut spending. My solution is to *abolish all personal and corporate federal income taxes.*

Income taxes not only hurt each of us personally, they restrict economic growth by constraining consumer spending. The partisan divide has perpetrated many myths that keep our nation from coming together on this issue. While the liberal party would have you believe that the wealthy are not paying their share of taxes, the conservative party would have you believe that nearly half of our citizens pay nothing in taxes. Surprising to many, the sting of taxes is a major issue for all of us, both rich and poor.

My platform stays true to my fiscally conservative roots when it comes to balancing the budget. I am absolutely against deficit spending. We need a balanced budget immediately, and not as a goal for somewhere down the road. Our deficit has wreaked havoc on the buying value of our dollar. Deficit spending, along with $18 trillion in accrued debt, are the reasons a young family starting out on a modest income can no longer afford to buy a house.

When my father graduated from college, he bought an acre of land and built a house by hand on his salary as a junior reporter for the *Miami News*. When I graduated from college, what my father had done was no longer possible on a starting salary, nor would the planning department allow anyone to build a house the way he had. Today's generation has it even harder, especially those graduating with a hundred thousand dollars in student debt.

Too many people think the deficit and national debt are abstract concepts that do not impact their personal lives. They absolutely impact your life—they erode your buying power every day. *The deficit and debt are the reasons that housing is so much less affordable today than it was in the past.*

I defy the conservative myth, however, when it comes to federal spending. We do not need to cut government spending to balance the budget. The myth of a bloated federal government is based upon our anecdotal experience of paying income taxes. Since the government takes a third or more of our income, it appears to us like a monstrous beast, devouring our personal resources. But if national security and retirement were to come at a miniscule cost, like I propose, our government would seem like a bargain.

These are radical concepts, but history is rich with ideas that were once radical and later became reality. When Tim Berners-Lee first proposed the web in 1989, for example, it was an outlandish idea. Today we cannot live without it. When Leonardo da Vinci invented flying machines, they were a fantasy. Today they define modern travel.

Think of the concepts in my platform as yet another breakthrough that advances civilization. My platform contains the upgrade code for our nation's outdated financial operating system; these are solutions that would make your life better.

MY POLITICAL PLATFORM

If the solutions I propose could be implemented simply by announcing them, I would write a book and retire to paint galaxies. Solutions, however, cannot be implemented through words alone. They must be fought for and defended, which is why I am running for President: to make these solutions a reality. I therefore make the following campaign promises to the people of America, if elected.

MY FIRST COMMITMENT is to eliminate income taxes, for both individuals and corporations, and replace them with a Financial Settlements Tax. This solution takes advantage of how the economy has changed since the Civil War, when income taxes were first used.

Today the primary source of revenue for our $3.9 trillion government budget is the $15 trillion we earn in income. Income, however, no longer represents the bulk of our economy as it once did. In the year 2013, there were over $4,456 trillion in financial settlements, dwarfing our $15 trillion in income. If we were to tax financial settlements instead of income, it would cost less than 0.1% per settlement to balance our budget.

Can you imagine not having to pay income taxes or Social Security taxes, and yet having the budget balanced? For example: if you earn $50,000 per year, you currently pay around $12,400 in federal taxes. With a Financial Settlements Tax, *you would only pay $50*.

MY SECOND COMMITMENT is to balance the budget. By tapping the vast amount of financial settlements in our nation, even at the miniscule rate of 0.1%, we can balance the budget without having to cut back on government spending. This is how we convert our government from a monstrous beast into a bargain.

My Third Commitment is to pay off the national debt. To accomplish this, I have developed a system called Coupon Stripping, which reverses the negative effect that Treasury bonds have had on our economy.

Under our current system, we use Treasury bonds to pay for our deficit. The problem, however, is that Treasury bonds are liquid; they serve as money in our economy and thus add to the money supply. Furthermore, because Treasury bonds earn interest, they compound the amount of debt we owe over time. To stop the compounding effect of interest and stabilize our money supply, we need to swap non-interest-bearing money for interest-bearing Treasury bonds.

Under Coupon Stripping, our nation could be debt-free in just five years. Furthermore, your savings would no longer erode over time because the value of the dollar would no longer decline year after year.

My Fourth Commitment is to enact Banking 2.0, eliminating interest in mortgages, student loans, and car loans, while increasing access to capital for small businesses and start-ups. This solution reconfigures our banking system, removing artificial barriers to capital and reducing the cost of finance.

Banking 2.0 removes the unnecessary costs that our current financial system imposes upon the economy. Under Banking 2.0, banks would become storefronts, or service agents, for the Federal Reserve. Banks would no longer hold deposits or lend depositors' funds. Instead, the repayment of deposits would be an obligation of the Fed, and the money for loans would come directly from the Fed.

Banks would no longer be permitted to charge interest for loans, nor would they have a cost of funds. Instead banks would charge a service fee for the origination and servicing of loans. Eliminating the cost of interest would have a profound effect on your cost of living; *the cost of buying a home would be cut nearly in half.*

IN ADDITION TO my four commitments, I outline a plan in the fifth chapter to capitalize growth through the use of Stimulus Payments, increasing production and employment without inflating the money supply. Capitalizing growth is the key to eliminating the mismatch between the ability of businesses to produce and the ability of consumers to buy. This mismatch is the result of a good thing—the increased productive efficiency of our material economy.

Because of technology and automation, the biggest challenge for businesses today is competing for customers. In the past, the biggest challenge was producing enough. We live in extraordinary times; we can produce as much as we want. The best thing we can do for businesses today is to provide more customers.

Stimulus Payments would entail creating new capital for distribution to citizens, thereby closing the gap between consumer spending and productive capacity. The distributed capital would then be removed from the money supply with the Financial Settlements Tax. When used in conjunction with a Financial Settlements Tax, Stimulus Payments are sustainable, boosting production and creating jobs.

I do not include Stimulus Payments as a commitment in my platform because we must implement my other solutions before we can determine how much to stimulate our economy. Eliminating income taxes, balancing the budget, and paying off our national debt will have a profound effect on our material economy, supercharging our production engine. Once we have implemented these solutions, we will be in a position to determine how much more growth we can capitalize through the use of Stimulus Payments.

Together, the solutions I propose are highly transformative. Perhaps someday they will lead to the world envisioned in *Star Trek* when Captain Jean-Luc Picard declared, "The economics of the future are somewhat different. You see, money doesn't exist in the 24th century," and Commander Deanna Troi chimed in,

"...poverty, disease, war—they'll all be gone within the next fifty years."[4]

Today, these solutions would unleash our nation's production engine, allowing us all to enjoy a life of greater abundance. They would free us from income taxes, create additional jobs, make it easier to start a business, reduce the cost of buying a home, and increase our disposable income. In short, the solutions I am proposing would transform our lives.

I am running for President because Americans deserve a better life. Together we can implement the operating system to make that happen. The time is right for real change. We have the technology; we just need to upgrade. We stand together at the precipice of what can be a new era of abundance—the dawning of the New American Dream.

---

[4] *Star Trek: First Contact*, © 1996 Paramount Pictures (All rights acknowledged).

CHAPTER TWO

WE ARE TAXING THE WRONG THING
Eliminating Income Taxes and the Deficit

"The hardest thing to understand in the world
is the income tax."
–Albert Einstein

HOW DO YOU feel about paying taxes? Do you remember your reaction to receiving your first paycheck and seeing how much had been deducted? I have hired several young people for their first jobs, and each of them has had the same reaction when receiving their first paycheck. First, they experience a feeling of accomplishment, followed by shock and dismay when they see the bite that taxes take out of their pay. They gasp, "There must be some mistake! Are you sure this is right?"

I then walk them through their payroll deductions. It is always a sobering experience. I remember one young woman who had just graduated from college looking at me with tears in her eyes and saying, "I thought I had it tough in college. Now I only have two weeks off each year, and so much of my pay is gone I can't afford what I thought I could." Later she said, "I finally appreciate my parents. I see how hard it's been for them."

Income Taxes are a financial burden for everyone, but we hunker down and pay them because we know we must. After all, we pay for cars, places to live, food, and clothing, so we accept that we also must pay for roads, schools, and national security.

Over time, many of us forget how much we pay in income taxes. We think of our salaries as being the net amount of our paychecks. In this chapter you will be reminded of how much you do pay in taxes—not to depress you, but to show you how much more you could have if we were to adopt a new means of paying for government spending.

"You don't pay taxes—they take taxes."
–Chris Rock

Taxation in a New Light—
Balancing the Money Supply

In 1913, the government gave the Federal Reserve the responsibility for printing and destroying money. In other words, the Fed manages our money supply.[5] One implication of the Fed's power is that *instead of taxing income, it is entirely possible for the Fed to print the money necessary to pay the government's bills.*

There is, of course, a glaring problem with this idea: if the Fed prints money to pay the government's bills, the money supply will mushroom and the dollar will plummet in value—*that is, unless we find a way to systematically evaporate the new money.* If we could somehow eliminate those dollars once the government has used them, the money supply would remain constant, and inflation would not occur.

There is a way to do this. It entails understanding taxation from a different perspective: realizing that taxation is merely a means of removing dollars from the money supply to make up for the dollars the government spends. Money is removed from the money supply when it is taxed, and it re-enters the money supply whenever the government makes a payment, whether it is a check to Lockheed for the acquisition of a missile, a social

---

[5] http://www.federalreserveeducation.org/about-the-fed/history/

security payment to a citizen in Iowa, or a wire transfer to China for interest on a Treasury bond.

The system I am proposing for balancing the budget treats money as if it were moving through the water cycle. Just as water flows across the landscape, government spending flows throughout the economy. The key is that water also evaporates; otherwise it would overfill the rivers, lakes, and oceans, resulting in flooding (inflation). Just as water evaporates to make way for more rainfall, money must evaporate to make way for new money.

> For every newly created dollar the government spends, another dollar must be removed from the money supply.

The problem with our current tax system is that *we only evaporate money from one source:* income. The water cycle works so well because evaporation occurs a little at a time throughout the entire system, not just from isolated sources. In the same way, taxes should come from the *entire* economy instead of just from Lake Income.

Imagine what would happen if the water for our nation's rainfall evaporated from a single lake. It would be catastrophic to the lake, and there would be a nation-wide drought. That is essentially how the government operates today; we pay high taxes that drain our personal resources, and we have a deficit. What we need is a means of distributing taxes evenly throughout our economy.

Instead of taxing our income, my solution is to evaporate *tiny* amounts of money from the abundance of transactions called "financial settlements," whose volume dwarfs income. I call this the Financial Settlements Tax (FST).

Essentially, a financial settlement is the process by which money changes hands. Anytime you deposit a check, sell a stock on Wall Street, or swipe your debit card at the grocery store, you have completed a financial settlement. Statistically speaking, the number of financial settlements that occur on a day-to-day basis far exceeds the amount we earn in income. Thus, taxing financial settlements would spread out the burden of government spending.

In the diagram of the Water Cycle below, evaporation balances rainfall.

EVAPORATION BALANCES THE WATER CYCLE

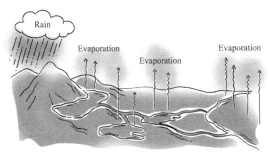

In the diagram of the Monetary Cycle below, the Federal Reserve creates the money that Congress spends. The same amount of money that the Fed creates is evaporated, or removed from the money supply, through the FST. This keeps the money supply balanced and puts a stop to our growing debt.

THE FST BALANCES THE MONETARY CYCLE

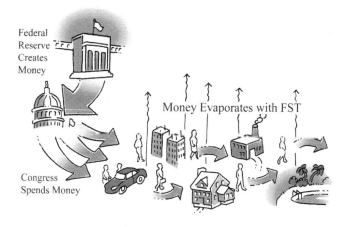

The diagram above illustrates how the FST would evaporate money broadly from the entire economy, rather than depleting a single source (income). That way, no one ends up losing.

How the Math Works

By primarily taxing income, we have selected far too narrow a category of economic transactions to tap. Personal income totals almost $15 trillion annually,[6] while the federal budget is $3.9 trillion per year.[7] Trying to extract $3.9 trillion from $15 trillion results in heavy taxes and a deficit.

Taxing income is one of those archaic constructs in our monetary system that leads to scarcity in the material economy, as consumer spending is critical to production. If we were to tap a much broader segment of our economy, such as financial settlements, we could greatly reduce the burden on any single taxpayer, and the monetary economy would foster abundance in the material economy. In fact, the math is so favorable that no taxpayer ends up being the loser.

Here is the short and sweet mathematical basis for taxing financial settlements. Settlements made through banks[8] and non-banks[9] (such as credit unions), plus

---

[6] The figure for personal income is rounded, based on December 31, 2014, and from
http://bea.gov/iTable/iTable.cfm?ReqID=9&step=1#reqid=9&step=3&isuri=1&903=58

[7] The figure for the federal budget is rounded, for the year 2015, from the White House budget summary, page 163, from http://www.whitehouse.gov/omb/budget.

[8] The Bank for International Settlements (bis.org) is an excellent source for data on settlements. Table 11 in the Committee on Payment and Settlement Systems' report, "Statistics on Payment Clearing and Settlement Systems in the CPSS Countries," published December 2014 (affectionately known as the Red Book), shows that settlements through the Clearing House

securities cleared,[10] totaled $4,456 trillion dollars in the year 2013.[11] *That is nearly 300 times the amount of our collective income.* Clearly, we are taxing the wrong thing!

Dividing the government's 2015 budget of $3.9 trillion by $4,456 trillion yields 0.0875%—the percentage that must be evaporated from each financial settlement in order to balance the budget. We will round that number up to 0.1%, a mere tenth of one percent, for the purposes of this book.

The Financial Settlements Tax is an astounding tool. At the low rate of 0.1%, the FST would eliminate the need for personal and corporate federal income taxes, Social Security taxes, Medicare taxes, unemployment taxes, estate and gift taxes—even excise and customs taxes—all of which cause much pain and

---

Interbank Payment System (CHIPS), Fedwire, checks, ACH, and on-us payments totaled $1,429 trillion in 2013.

[9] Table 8 in the Red Book shows that the use of payment instruments, ACH, cards and checks by non-banks totaled $92 trillion in 2013.

[10] Table 21 in the Red Book shows that the value of contracts and transactions cleared at the National Securities Clearing Corporation, the Fixed Income Clearing Corporation, the Government Securities Division, and the Mortgage-Backed Securities Division totaled $2,517 trillion in 2013. Table 26 in the Red Book shows transactions cleared at the Depository Trust Company and the Federal Reserve totaled $418 trillion in 2013.

[11] The figures of $1,429 trillion from Table 11, $92 trillion from Table 8, $2,517 trillion from Table 21 and $418 trillion from Table 26, total $4,456 trillion for the year 2013.

yet fall hundreds of billions of dollars short of balancing the budget.

> Instead of paying up to $400 in taxes on $1,000 of income, you would pay only $1. And instead of a half trillion-dollar deficit, the budget would be balanced.

The graph below compares the amount of income in our nation (the thin black line) to the amount of financial settlements (the large gray area). It is clear we are taxing the wrong thing.

INCOME VERSUS FINANCIAL SETTLEMENTS

Contrast our federal budget (black) with our national income (gray) in the first diagram. Then compare our federal budget (the black sliver) to the total amount of financial settlements (the large gray area) in the second diagram. Once again, it is apparent that we have been taxing the wrong thing.

THE FEDERAL BUDGET COMPARED TO INCOME

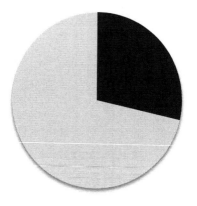

THE FEDERAL BUDGET COMPARED TO FINANCIAL SETTLEMENTS

The next two illustrations compare income taxes to the Financial Settlements Tax from yet another perspective.

Why Income Taxes Are So Expensive
Paying $3.9 trillion from a $15 trillion bucket

WHY THE FST IS SO INEXPENSIVE
Paying $3.9 trillion from a $4,456 trillion tank

The reason the Financial Settlements Tax works, and the reason it is painless, is that it taps every settlement. Only a tiny fraction of settlements are taxed today—those settlements that we deem to be "income." With the FST, we are primarily taxing the burgeoning monetary economy. Essentially, we are exacting a tiny squeak from an enormous balloon (the financial sector) that dwarfs the material economy you and I live in.

Fortunately, the caretakers of that balloon are people like you and me, so they will benefit from the Financial Settlements Tax just as we will. In fact, the balloon itself is so large that the FST will barely have any effect on it.

The FST is a prime example of how we can engineer the monetary economy to *benefit* the material economy, rather than having the monetary economy create *barriers* for the material economy, as it does now. The result is a smaller bite out of your paycheck.

What the FST Would Mean to You

What would the Financial Settlements Tax mean for you personally? As we continue to explore the solutions in this book, we will examine the benefits of each solution for individual citizens. For this purpose, we will track the effect of each solution on several hypothetical characters:

- Tom, in his early twenties, feels fortunate to earn $30k per year. He has some credit card debt, is considering college, and aspires to be an entrepreneur.

- Amanda, a professional in her early thirties, earns $50k per year, has student loans and credit card debt, and is hoping to buy a home.

- Jennifer and Joe, married professionals in their early forties with a combined income of $100k, have two children and own a home. They pay student loans, a mortgage, and credit card debt.

TOM

Life with Income Taxes

$ 30,000
−$ 6,290
$ 23,710

Life with the FST

"I have an extra $6k with the FST."

$ 30,000
−$ 30
$ 29,970

Let us consider the effect the Financial Settlements Tax would have on each of these characters. Tom would pay just $30 per year with the FST, compared to over $6k in income taxes and Social Security taxes, boosting his net income by 26%. For Tom, the extra $6k per year in net pay would be a game changer, allowing him to take classes at his local community college to learn how to start his own business.

Life with Income Taxes

$ 50,000
−$ 12,489
$37,511

Life with the FST

"I have an extra $12k with the FST."

$50,000
−$ 50
$49,950

Amanda's tax bill of $12k would be reduced to just $50 with the FST, boosting her net pay by 33%. Amanda could save $10k each year for a down payment on a home and still have an extra $2k annually in disposable income.

Life with Income Taxes

Life with the FST

$100,000
–$ 22,574
$77,426

"We have an extra
$22k with the FST."

$100,000
–$ 100
$99,900

The $22k that Jennifer and Joe pay in taxes is a significant burden, especially with two children. Reducing the payment to just $100 with the FST would substantially increase their net income. With the extra money Jennifer and Joe could spend $5k annually on family vacations, invest $15k per year in a college fund for their children, and still have $2k left over.

The calculations for our characters' income taxes and Social Security taxes were derived from IRS tax tables and were calculated based upon certain assumptions. [12] Although the actual figures for each

---

[12] Tom and Amanda's taxes were calculated as follows: income – $5,950 standard deduction – $3,800 personal exemption = value applied to tax table, plus income x .9235 x .133 per Form SE for Social Security tax. Jennifer and Joe's taxes were calculated as follows: gross income of $100,000 – $11,900 standard deduction – ($3,800 x 4 exemptions) = a tax of $10,291 based on the Form 1040 tax table, plus $100,000 x .9235 x .133 based on the Form SE for Social Security tax. No deduction was taken for

person will vary, it is easy to see how powerful a solution the FST would be for increasing your net income.

WHAT THE FST WOULD MEAN TO OUR NATION

Because the Financial Settlements Tax would put more money in everyone's pocket, consumer spending would increase and our nation's Gross Domestic Production (GDP) would rise. Since businesses would no longer pay corporate or FICA taxes, they would have more money to expand and hire new employees. And because our government would be operating in the black, our national debt would no longer skyrocket. Together, these factors would propel our economy to new heights. But the benefits of the FST go well beyond this.

Under the Financial Settlements Tax, companies would no longer use foreign subsidiaries to hide from U.S. taxes, as foreign tax rates are higher than the FST. Likewise, the problem of "inversions," or companies moving their headquarters offshore, would be solved with the FST. Instead, we would see a return of the dollars that multinational companies currently stash offshore, which would increase the volume of financial settlements in our nation. Eliminating income taxes

---

mortgage interest, as it was assumed to be equal or less than the standard deduction.

would also bring a flood of money from foreign corporations and individuals into our country, resulting in increased investment in our economy and even more financial settlements. In short, the U.S. would become an international tax haven.

Finally, the Financial Settlements Tax would save Social Security. According to current Social Security Administration estimates, trust funds supplementing the payment of Social Security benefits will be exhausted in a dozen years. At that time, benefits to retirees will need to be cut and/or FICA tax rates increased.[13] In other words, the Social Security program is already insolvent, with expenditures exceeding receipts; it is currently in its final stages of unraveling. The FST would eliminate this ticking time bomb, bringing solvency to our Social Security program.

If you are retired, the Financial Settlements Tax would allow you to continue receiving benefits without fear of losing them in the future. If you are young, the FST would protect you from higher FICA taxes and ensure that Social Security will still be around when you reach retirement age.

In summary, the overall effect of the Financial Settlements Tax is that our economy would boom, and you and I would be better off financially. The FST is a simple solution for what once seemed to be an

---

[13] http://www.ssa.gov/policy/docs/ssb/v70n3/v70n3p111.html

intractable problem. We no longer need to suffer the pain of high taxes and deficit spending. Instead, we have a non-partisan solution in which we all win, with everyone contributing a tiny portion of each financial settlement that we make. It is a solution similar to the way we each painlessly contribute to the evaporation that is necessary for rainfall when we drink a glass of water.

Could the FST Replace State and Local Taxes?

Just as it is surprisingly inexpensive to replace federal taxes with a Financial Settlements Tax, it is also feasible to replace state and local taxes with the FST. State and local income taxes, property taxes, and sales taxes totaled $1.3 trillion in 2013.[14] If the tax rate on financial settlements was set at 0.12%, we could not only eliminate federal income taxes, but we could also eliminate state and local taxes. In other words, simply by debiting $1.20 every time a $1,000 deposit is made in a bank or credit union, or a security is sold on Wall Street, we would no longer have to pay state and local income taxes, property taxes, or sales taxes.

It is likely that such a proposal would be popular with a number of states, especially if state rights were

---

[14] https://www.census.gov/govs/qtax/historical_data.html

not impacted. The easiest way to accomplish this would be for the Federal Reserve to make a flat disbursement to each state based solely upon the state's population. Whether or not a state elected to charge its citizens additional taxes would be left up to the state.

Using the Financial Settlements Tax to eliminate state and local taxes is not one of my campaign commitments, however. Such a proposal would need to come from the states, and only once the FST had been successfully implemented at the federal level.

IMPLEMENTING THE FST

The Financial Settlements Tax would be relatively easy to implement, insofar as government programs go. It would not require the creation of new government agencies, nor would it require 73,954 pages of complex tax code, as our current system does.[15]

The Financial Settlements Tax would involve a single adjustment to the clearing process for financial institutions: if you deposited a check for $1,000 into your bank account, for example, the bank would only credit you $999.[16] Because the bank deleted $1 from your deposit, you would no longer have to file IRS

---

[15] The page count is obsolete almost the moment you write it. For an up-to-date count see: http://www.cch.com/TaxLawPileUp.pdf

[16] The FST would occur only when you make deposits, and not when you make withdrawals.

forms, nor would you have federal payroll taxes withheld from your paycheck.

The $1 that is not credited to your account would not go to the bank, nor would it be sent to the government; it would simply "evaporate." Thus the money not credited to your account would be removed from the money supply, simply because it is no longer on *anyone's* balance sheet. Because this money evaporates continually, the Fed would be free to print new money, paying for government spending without causing inflation. The Financial Settlements Tax is a way to destroy money, making room for the new money being created by the Fed to pay for government spending.

> The process of not crediting a portion of a deposit to any account deletes that money from the money supply.

The $1 would be debited because you engaged in a financial settlement when you deposited your $1,000 check. Remember: depositing a check, receiving a wire, or receiving money from the sale of stock are all examples of financial settlements. In short, any money received by anyone is a financial settlement. Most people, when they hear the plan for a Financial Settlements Tax, assume it is the banks that will be up in arms over the FST, but that is not so. The money is not coming from the banks; it is coming directly from customers.

ENFORCING THE FST

The Financial Settlements Tax would be easier to enforce and more difficult to game than income taxes. In large measure, the feasibility of enforcement is tied to the party responsible for compliance, which is why we require employers to withhold taxes rather than relying on employees to make payments on their own.

With the FST, the government would look to highly regulated institutions to evaporate transactions, and evaporation would be an automatic part of the clearing of financial settlements, whether the institution is a bank, a non-bank such as a credit union, or a securities clearinghouse. Notably, the payer from whose funds the FST is deducted would not have any say in the process.

The feasibility of enforcement is also tied to the pain of compliance. Whereas federal income taxes deduct 20–40% of personal income, the cost of the Financial Settlements Tax would be miniscule, so the incentive to avoid the FST would be far lower than the incentive to avoid income taxes.

Person-to-person cash transactions would avoid evaporation, of course, just as they are a means of avoiding income taxes today. Such transactions are impossible to track, and their volume is tiny compared to the size of the economy, so for this reason I have excluded them from the Financial Settlements Tax.

I have had some very interesting reactions when talking to people about the Financial Settlements Tax.

One analyst at the Fed expressed her concern that people would stop depositing checks with the FST.

"What would they do with their checks if they don't deposit them?" I asked.

"I don't know, but they'll game the system," she insisted. "They'll make their employers pay them in cash."

"Do you really think they'll do that to save 0.1% when they don't ask for cash to avoid payroll taxes of 30% or more?" I asked. "And look at the fees that the banks charge. Three dollars for an ATM withdrawal; the FST is lower than that!"

She paused and shook her head, "I just don't think people will put up with it."

"And the taxes that we pay are easier to put up with?" I asked.

As I thought through that conversation, I realized how easy it is to settle for things the way they are, and how hard it is to change. We are so easily trapped into lives of quiet desperation. We cannot let our nation die of quiet desperation.

THE PAIN OF A CENTURY OF INCOME TAXES

During President Lincoln's administration, the government's need for revenue increased sharply because of the Civil War. By temporarily imposing a small tax on the income of the wealthy, the government was able to cover its expenses.[17] After the Civil War, the idea of permanently taxing income was vigorously debated for decades. In 1913, income taxes became a permanent fixture of the government's revenue plan; again, a small percentage of the income of the wealthiest citizens was taxed.

That soon changed, however, and tax rates fluctuated wildly for the next century.[18] The tax rate for the wealthiest skyrocketed from 7% in 1913 all the way to 77% in just five years. You can imagine the outcry that caused. High rates for the wealthy remained in place for years, until they briefly fell to 24% in 1929. They bounced back almost immediately with the Great Depression, reaching 63% in 1932, and then climbed ever higher for a full decade until they hit 94% in 1942.

Rates remained at this level for 22 years, barely fluctuating, until they were reduced to 77% in 1964. This was followed by yet another reduction a year later, to 70%, where they remained for 17 years. President

---

[17] www.taxhistory.org, www.archives.gov, www.civilwar.org

[18] www.taxpolicycenter.org, www.cch.com, www.taxfoundation.org, and http://qz.com/74271/income-tax-rates-since-1913/

Reagan dropped the rate for the wealthy to 50% in 1982, followed by further reductions until they hit a low of 28% in 1988. In 1991 President Bush edged rates up to 31%, followed by a hike to 39.6% by President Clinton in 1993. Finally, ten years later, rates edged back down to 35%.

It is surprising to many that for most of the past century, tax rates for the wealthy have been much higher than they are today. In fact, unless we adopt a radically different means of paying for government spending, history indicates that tax rates are likely to increase. This is sobering news for anyone who believes that the sting of government taxes is a recent development and could be reduced if we just returned to "the good old days."

If you think we are imposing hefty taxes today, and are concerned that we have a deficit, tomorrow will be worse. The pain we feel from this is polarizing our nation. It causes us to point fingers and let conflicting accusations fly: "the rich aren't paying their fair share"; "the poor aren't paying their fair share"; "the government spends too much"; and "the government needs to spend more to get us out of this mess."

The problem with this way of thinking is that we are pre-supposing pain as a given. The truth is that we are suffering from an artificial barrier to greater prosperity that can be removed once we understand the root of the problem. In fact, the solution is neither paying higher income taxes nor cutting government spending.

Once we understand how our economy has changed since the civil war, we see that the solution comes in an entirely different form—the Financial Settlements Tax. We have simply been taxing the wrong thing. We no longer need to shoulder the burden of income taxes.

"The marvel of all history is the patience with which men and women submit to burdens unnecessarily laid upon them by their governments."
–George Washington

CHAPTER THREE

ELIMINATING THE NATIONAL DEBT
Securing Your Financial Future

"Will I obliterate the national debt? Sure, why not?"
–Pat Paulsen, comedian

WITH A SOLUTION in hand for eliminating income taxes and balancing the budget, let us look at what we can do about paying off our national debt.

OUR SKYROCKETING NATIONAL DEBT

Trillions

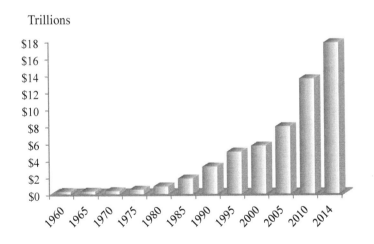

As you can see in the graph on the previous page, our government has consistently spent more money than it collects in taxes, thus racking up our national debt. Our debt took on epic proportions in the 1980s and has doubled every ten years since then.[19] Today, years of deficit spending have left us with an astonishing $18 trillion in debt, amounting to $57,000 for every man, woman, and child in the country.[20] If the graph seems unsustainable, it is.

The government currently makes up the difference between what it collects in taxes and what it spends by selling Treasury bonds.[21] The money the government receives from the sale of Treasury bonds provides the additional money the government needs to cover the cost of its operations; in other words, the government borrows to pay for its deficit spending. Our national debt is the total amount of Treasury bonds outstanding.

Treasury bonds are simply IOUs, or a promise on behalf of our government to repay the money it has borrowed. Unfortunately, however, the government currently has no plan to repay the money it has

---

[19]   http://www.treasurydirect.gov/govt/reports/pd/histdebt/histdebt.htm (source of data in the graph). See http://www.usadebtclock.com for a real-time view of the debt.

[20] http://www.treasurydirect.gov/NP/debt/current. National debt as of December 2014. Per capita figure is based on a population of 315 million.

[21] For two good sources of history on Treasury bonds, visit either: http://www.treasurydirect.gov/indiv/research/history/histtime/histtime_bon ds.htm, http://www.gao.gov/special.pubs/longterm/debt/index.html

borrowed.[22] The national debt is therefore climbing with no end in sight.

If we replaced income taxes with the Financial Settlements Tax, the national debt's growth would be stopped in its tracks. Our government would no longer need to sell Treasury bonds to cover the deficit because the budget would be balanced.

However, while the FST solves the problem of our spiraling debt, we need a different solution to repay debt incurred in the past. Fortunately, like the deficit, the debt is the result of a flaw in our monetary system that can be corrected, and our debt can be paid off in a way that will actually help the material economy. The answer is to replace our nation's "bad money" with "good money," using a process that I call "Coupon Stripping."

GOOD MONEY VERSUS BAD MONEY

The Treasury bonds that the government sells devalue the dollar because Wall Street "monetizes" Treasury bonds. Think of Wall Street as a system for making stocks and bonds liquid, or converting them into cash; thanks to this process, Treasury bonds become the same as money. Thus, when we flood the money supply with Treasury bonds, we devalue the dollar just as if we were flooding the money supply with newly printed currency.

---

[22] http://www.whitehouse.gov/omb/budget

In essence, we have created two forms of money: ordinary currency and Treasury bonds. The only real difference is that Treasury bonds earn interest—which is exactly what makes them problematic.

Let me provide an illustration. Not long ago, the government issued a form of Treasury bond called a "bearer bond." It was called this because it could be transferred by hand from one person to another, just like currency. In other words, whoever was the "bearer" owned the bond. No record was kept of the transfer of ownership. Bearer bonds were even printed on green paper, making them all the more like money.

I know this because I once owned a bearer bond, courtesy of my grandfather. The similarity between the bearer bond and currency planted a seed in my mind that eventually led to Coupon Stripping as a solution for our national debt. Take a look at the illustration below. The only difference between the $100 bill on the left and the $100 bearer bond on the right is that coupons surround the $100 on the right.

CURRENCY VERSUS TREASURY BONDS
(Good Money Versus Bad Money)

Good Money   Bad Money

Bearer bonds worked like this: every time a coupon matured, the owner clipped it off and redeemed it for cash at the bank. A new coupon matured every six months. Bearer bonds were nifty.

I remember asking grandfather, "What's the difference between bearer bonds and money, other than the coupons?" He answered, "Nothing. It's better to own bearer bonds than cash because bearer bonds *grow*." And therein lies the problem with interest: it makes our money supply grow. Because Treasury bonds (like bearer bonds) earn interest and contribute to inflation, they are "bad" money.

When my grandfather told me that the national debt increased not only because of the deficit we incurred each year, but also because of the interest on Treasury bonds, I thought, "That's dumb. We should just print regular money to pay for the debt instead of Treasury bonds." I kept silent, though, because I figured there must be a good reason for Treasury bonds. Now I know better, which is why I am running for President.

Then my grandfather told me about inflation. He recalled the rising price of bread over the years, and he reminisced about the prices that various houses in the neighborhood had sold for in the past. I remember thinking, "When will it end?"

The cost of a four-year Ivy League education had topped $10,000 in the '70's, when I attended college, and people were appalled. At that time, I extrapolated the increase in tuition and was stunned to see that four years of tuition would top $200,000 by the time I had children in college. That figure seemed as preposterous then as $4 million for college seems to us today—but both are merely 20-fold increases.

Imagine paying $4 million to go to college. Imagine a loaf of bread costing $60. You can see why saving for retirement today is so futile. Today's money is worth nothing tomorrow.

Inflation erodes the middle class and creates a greater divide between rich and poor, as the rich tend to own assets that appreciate with inflation. Such a system is not sustainable. Our current cycle of recessions merely foreshadows a greater financial collapse. Like our present Social Security system, our growing debt is a ticking time bomb.

HOW COUPON STRIPPING WORKS

The irony is that, in the end, we all pay the very taxes we were trying to avoid by borrowing. We pay them indirectly, when the buying power of the dollar declines due to inflation. Treasury bonds are the reason a loaf of bread cost three dollars today instead of ten cents as it once did.[23]

---

[23] http://www.thepeoplehistory.com/70yearsofpricechange.html

1940   Today

Inflation is an increase in the cost of goods and services over time, occurring when too much money enters the money supply. Because Treasury bonds are a form of money, they add to the money supply, which increases the cost of goods and services and reduces the value of the dollar. Because Treasury bonds earn interest, they continue to add to the money supply as long as they remain in existence, further reducing the value of the dollar.

The FST takes care of the root of the problem, as it halts the growth of debt by eliminating the deficit. Paying off the debt that piled up in the past turns out to be even easier. I call the solution "Coupon Stripping" because it strips the interest coupons from Treasury bonds.

Coupon Stripping entails the substitution of non-interest-bearing money for interest-bearing money (Treasury bonds), effectively paying off our accrued national debt without further inflating the money supply. Coupon Stripping relies on the fact that the damage to our money supply has already been done. The money supply was inflated when the Treasury bonds were issued. Prices are what they are today because of what we did in the past. We have already paid for our past economic sins. We do not need to keep adding to those sins with interest.

Under Coupon Stripping, the Federal Reserve would pay off Treasury bonds on a scheduled basis by issuing new currency, which does not bear interest (i.e. "good money"), and using it to buy Treasury bonds, which do bear interest (i.e. "bad money").

Is this simply a form of printing money? Yes, it absolutely is. But it is not inflationary, because it replaces interest-bearing money with non-interest-bearing money. Under Coupon Stripping, the Federal Reserve would not keep the Treasury bonds it purchases on its books as it does now under its Quantitative Easing program; *it would cancel the Treasury bonds it purchases,* as they need to be permanently removed from the money supply.

Ironically, we would have inflated the money supply far less if we had simply issued new money to pay for the deficit every year, rather that selling Treasury bonds. At least ordinary money does not accrue interest.

T-Bonds Cause the Money Supply To Expand over Time

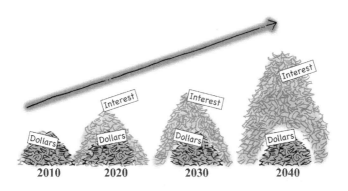

Converting T-Bonds to Dollars Stops the Expansion

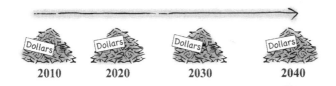

Paying Off Our Debt

How long would it take to pay off our debt with Coupon Stripping? The problem with paying off the entire debt in a single payment, which I wish we could do, is that the amount of our national debt is too great to be redeployed in new investments all at once. The schedule for repayment, therefore, must be such that it permits the redeployment of the money invested in Treasury bonds without disrupting the capital markets.

In essence, the money tied up in Treasury bonds is currently parked, doing nothing for our economy but accruing interest and inflating the money supply. The redeployment of the money invested in Treasury bonds, therefore, is one of the greatest opportunities for economic growth our nation has ever had. My solution for national debt transforms a long-standing problem into a grand opportunity.

The following three-phase plan for Coupon Stripping is based on first eliminating the debt owed to agencies within the U.S. government and the Federal Reserve, then eliminating the debt owed to foreign entities, and finally eliminating the debt owed within our nation. Our nation could be debt-free in just five years.

Phase 1: About $5.1 trillion of our nation's debt is owned by various trust funds *within* the U.S. government, such as the Social Security Administration, in the form of Treasury bonds.[24] We could pay off this portion of the debt without having to create any new money at all.

Because the FST would eliminate the deficit, the bonds that the government agency trust funds now rely upon for additional income *would no longer be necessary*. The Treasury bonds in the trust funds could thus be cancelled without any ill effect.

---

[24] http://www.treasurydirect.gov/NP/debt/current shows how much of the debt is held by entities within the government. The figure of $5.1 trillion is as of December 2014.

Another $2.5 trillion of the national debt is held in the form of Treasury bonds owned by the Federal Reserve.[25] Under Quantitative Easing, the Fed has been buying Treasury bonds, along with other bonds, which the Fed keeps on its balance sheet for resale. This means the bonds that the Fed purchases under Quantitative Easing remain a part of the money supply, and that they continue to earn interest.

Quantitative Easing was designed to stimulate economic growth, but it does so at the expense of inflating the money supply. Because the FST would stimulate economic growth (by eliminating income taxes) without inflating the money supply (because there would no longer be a deficit), Quantitative Easing would no longer be necessary.

The Treasury bonds owned by the Fed could be cancelled in the same manner as the Treasury bonds owned by the government agency trust funds. This would not only pay off the $2.5 trillion in debt that the Treasury Department owes the Fed, but it would also relieve the bloating of the money supply that happens when Treasury bonds are held on the Fed's balance sheet.

These two accounting moves would instantly reduce our debt from $18 trillion to $10.4 trillion. It is

---

[25]   http://www.newyorkfed.org/markets/soma/sysopen_accholdings.html shows the debt owned by the Fed. The figure of $2.5 trillion is as of December 2014.

quite astounding to realize that our government's largest creditor is *itself!* Fortunately this makes the problem easier to solve.

Phase 2: The next logical step would be to pay off the portion of our national debt owed to foreign entities. Foreign entities own about $6 trillion of our debt.[26] One of the main reasons China and Japan buy U.S. Treasury bonds is to keep our dollar strong, as that keeps the price of their exports low. Therefore, repaying our debt to foreign nations at the rate of $2 trillion per year, over a three-year period, would not be inflationary.

Phase 3: As a final step in eliminating our debt, we could pay off the remaining $4.4 trillion of debt that our nation owes to individual U.S. citizens, state and local governments, pension funds, money market funds, banks, and mutual funds. They would re-invest the proceeds from repayment, which would serve to capitalize economic growth. Once repayment of the foreign debt is complete, the debt held domestically could be repaid at the rate of $2.2 trillion per year over two years.

---

[26] The figure of $6 trillion is as of December 2014 and can be found at the following site: http://www.treasury.gov/resource-center/data-chart-center/tic/Documents/mfh.txt.

How Coupon Stripping Would Pay Off the National Debt

Trillions

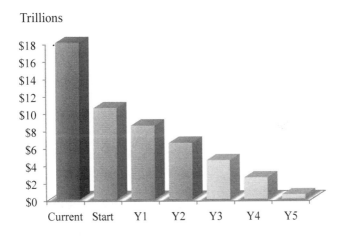

	Phase 1	Phase 2	Phase 3
	Paying off the debt owned internally by government agency trust funds could commence immediately upon the adoption of the FST.	Paying off the foreign-owned debt would take 3 years	Paying off the debt owned by U.S. citizens and entities would take 2 years

Should We Downsize Our Money Supply?

Coupon Stripping begs the question of whether we should use the Financial Settlements Tax to pare back the money supply. The answer is: it depends on which direction we want to move the value of the dollar. Do we want to erase some of the past erosion in the buying power of the dollar, or are we better off keeping the dollar's buying power where it is?

Because we would enjoy greater economic growth with a lower tax rate for the Financial Settlements Tax, it is probably best to leave the money supply at its current size. We have already paid for our past mistakes through inflation, and there is little to gain in trying to reverse it. A change in the value of the dollar, either up or down, is a two-edged sword. While increasing the value of the dollar by evaporating the repayment of debt would decrease the cost of foreign goods, which would give the American consumer more for their money, it would also decrease the volume of exports for American firms.

The good news is that Coupon Stripping does not add to the budget or to the money supply, as it entails exchanging one form of money for another. If we want to keep the dollar stable, therefore, the amount of money exchanged by the Federal Reserve for Treasury bonds should *not* be included in calculating the rate for the Financial Settlements Tax. Coupon Stripping is not a part of the government's budget; instead, it is a function of the Federal Reserve for balancing the money supply, which can be implemented at no cost to the taxpayer.

Once we have identified the artificial barriers to the repayment of our national debt, the solution itself is almost anticlimactic. Within five years of implementing Coupon Stripping, our nation would be the only major debt-free, deficit-free, and income tax-free nation in the world. Our economy would be the envy of all, and your future would have a more secure financial foundation than it does today.

"I am a firm believer in the people. If given the truth, they can be depended upon to meet any national crisis. The great point is to bring them the real facts."
–Abraham Lincoln

CHAPTER FOUR

BANKING 2.0
Cutting the Cost of Finance

"A bank is a place that will lend you money if you can prove that you don't need it."
–Bob Hope, comedian

THE ORIGIN OF our banking system, like the origin of our tax system, is rooted in the days when we used gold as money. And like our current tax system, certain aspects of today's banking system hinder the progress of our modern economy, negatively impacting each of us individually.

> Our problem is that we are trying to run a 21st century economy on a 19th century operating system.

When we used gold as money, banks ensured there was sufficient gold to facilitate transactions in the material economy. Thus banks became "aggregators of money." And when money was gold, it was expensive to aggregate money, which led to the concept that there is a "cost of funds."

To cover overhead and earn profits, banks invested the deposits they received—usually in the form of loans. By doing so, banks made enough money to pay their depositors interest and earn a profit. That is how banks came to be in the business of "making money off of money." Instead of selling products and services, as is done in the material economy, banks sell money. This is how the monetary economy was born.

THE FRICTION OF ARCHAIC BANKING TODAY

Today, banks still aggregate money in order to do business, which they do by accepting deposits and selling stock. The truth, however, is that we no longer need banks to aggregate money because the authority to create dollars and manage our money supply has been given to the Federal Reserve.[27]

---

[27] http://www.federalreserve.gov/pf/pdf/pf_1.pdf#page=4.

Under our current system, banks are also required to have a certain amount of equity on hand, and the ratio of a bank's loans to its deposits is regulated. This needlessly burdens the economy, and it increases our cost of living. It also gives large banks an advantage over small banks.

Modern banks have been released from the overhead they bore in the 19th century, when they had to transport and distribute gold. Likewise, banks enjoy increased efficiency through advances in technology, such as the Internet and automated teller machines. Mostly, however, these benefits have not been passed on to customers. If they were, it would have a profound effect on the material economy, dramatically improving our standard of living.

Instead, banking has ballooned to the point that the financial sector profits from synthetic transactions having nothing to do with the real world, with notional values exceeding the gross production of the entire planet.[28] Today, the financial sector garners 30–40% of our nation's corporate profits. [29] This level of profitability is not good for our economy.

Remember, the role of the monetary economy is to facilitate growth in the material economy, not deplete it of resources. *Any excess money we invest in the*

---

[28] http://www.bis.org/statistics/derstats.htm

[29] From bea.gov data; see the chart at http://blogs.reuters.com/felix-salmon/2011/03/30/chart-of-the-day-us-financial-profits/

financial sector unnecessarily saps production and increases our cost of living. Excess in the banking industry serves as friction, devouring the production of our material economy.

Rather than impeding growth in this way, we want banks to stoke the production engine in our material economy, keeping it robust. This would shrink the gap between rich and poor and help re-establish our nation's middle class.

THE BASIS FOR BANKING 2.0

How might the banking system better serve our economy? We still need banks to provide financial services, of course. But it no longer serves us to have banks making money off of money. Instead, it is best that our banking system create as little friction as possible in the material economy.

Under Banking 2.0, banks would act as financial servicers: originating and underwriting loans, servicing loans, foreclosing on collateral in the event of defaults, liquidating foreclosed properties, managing lines of credit, and doing essentially everything they do now— except that they would be doing all of this *as intermediaries for the Federal Reserve.*

Instead of making money off of the money they manage, banks would earn servicing fees from their customers. And because banks would obtain their money directly from the Fed, rather than depending upon equity and deposits, little banks would be able to compete with big banks, helping to reduce service fees for customers.

Borrowing from a bank would still cost money due to origination and service fees, and of course you would still have to pay back the loan, but you would *no longer pay interest on the loan*, so loans would cost substantially less than they do today. Deposits would no longer bear interest, either, because deposits would be a credit established with the Fed and not money you have entrusted to the bank for the purpose of lending.

An analogy for Banking 2.0 came to me recently as I was flying across the country, watching city after city go by and reflecting on the efforts of the municipal water departments to secure water. What would it be like if we could issue water like we issue money? Would we still require the water department to dig wells, dam rivers, and build expensive pipelines? That would make no sense. Why add unnecessarily to the cost of water?

"It is the same for banks," I thought. I recalled the people I knew who had started banks. Sourcing the money to capitalize a bank and garnering deposits was a major effort and expense. The cost of the bank's capital added to the inherent cost of running the bank, which was passed on to the borrower.

The irony is that we issue money through the Fed, so there is no reason to charge for capital, just as there would be no reason to require the water department to dig wells if we could create water right at people's sinks. It does not benefit us for banks to lend and invest money that they pay for, as that drives the cost of financial services up. We would be better served if banks were service agents, or storefronts, for the Federal Reserve, and their only purpose was to facilitate financial transactions in the material economy.

We no longer need banks to be aggregators of money since the Fed is the source of our money. Under the system I am proposing, the Fed would be an *agency* under the control of our government; it would cease to be an unaudited, privately held entity, as it is today. We collectively own our public lands. We should collectively own our central bank.

If banks served as the interface between the Federal Reserve and customers, it would obviate the need for imposing lending limits based upon the size of a bank's equity base.[30] Instead, banks would make loans on behalf of the Fed, and a little bank would have the same lending power as a big bank.

This would provide a more flexible and cost-efficient lending system and would eliminate the possibility of bank failures and the subsequent loss of customers' deposits. Because banks would be intermediaries for the Fed, merely servicing a customer's deposit, the deposit would actually be a credit with the Fed itself. Thus the customer would be relying on the Fed's ability to return their deposit, not the bank's balance sheet.

Banking 2.0 is not only good for the customer, it is also good for the banker. The relationship I propose between the Federal Reserve and our nation's banks would give banks substantially more financial power than they have today. Our banks would be able to provide international finance on an unprecedented level, vastly strengthening our global influence and further improving our nation's economy. Banking 2.0 is a win-win for everyone.

---

[30] A bank's equity is the amount of money that the shareholders have invested in the bank, plus any retained earnings. The amount of equity a bank has increases its lending capacity, thus bigger banks have an advantage over little banks in competing for loans.

HOW THE MATH WORKS

Banking 2.0 is a powerful concept with the potential to do more for our collective wherewithal than any of the other solutions in this book. The elimination of interest alone would:

- Drop the monthly payment on a $400,000 mortgage from $2,147 to $1,111, saving $372,960.[31]

- Drop the monthly payment on $100,000 in student debt from $763 to $417, saving $83,040.[32]

---

[31] The higher payment is calculated at 5% interest with a 30-year amortization. The lower payment is 0% interest, same amortization.

[32] The higher payment is calculated at 6.8% interest with a 20-year amortization. The lower payment is 0% interest, same amortization.

- Drop the monthly payment on $50,000 in credit card debt from $901 to $417, saving $58,080.[33]

Banking 2.0 would not be a free-for-all for the customer, as the usual lending parameters would stay in place. One could not borrow their way to a life of wealth without earning it. Credit would cost less, however, meaning that the money saved in each of the above examples could be used to buy goods and services instead. This illustrates just how burdensome the practice of charging interest is to each of individually as well as to our economy.

BANKS AS PROVIDERS OF DEPOSITORY SERVICES AND LENDERS

Under Banking 2.0, the safekeeping of deposits and the business of making loans would work as follows:

- Banks would accept deposits as intermediaries of the Federal Reserve and would no longer count deposits as a liability, nor would depositors look to the bank as the source of repayment of their deposits. Instead, the Fed would be responsible for the repayment of deposits.

---

[33] The higher payment is calculated at 18% interest with a 10-year amortization. The lower payment is 0% interest, same amortization.

- Banks would originate and service loans as intermediaries of the Fed, charging fees for their services but no longer charging interest on loans. The Fed would serve as the source of funds for bank loans, providing capital to the bank on an interest-free basis and setting the underwriting and servicing criteria for lending.

- Banks could specialize in providing either depository or lending services, since they would no longer be matching loans against deposits. Banks would not have balance sheets as they now do, nor would their solvency be based upon how their loans perform compared to the cost of their deposits.

BANKS AS INVESTORS

Banking 2.0 can meet a broader range of our financial needs than our current banking system, providing private equity and venture capital. There is historical precedence for banks to provide a wider range of services than they do today. The Medici family of Florence, Italy, for example, was a legendary family of bankers that helped launch the Renaissance by financing business, trade, venture, the arts, the church, and even public works.[34] Similarly, in the 18th and 19th centuries, England's banks not only financed trade but also the

---

[34] http://www.economist.com/node/347333

development of infrastructure in colonies, which transformed the world.[35]

Under Banking 2.0, banks would make equity investments in private and public companies, PE funds, and REITs, investing alongside pension funds, insurance companies, and private investors. While a bank's loans would not earn interest, a bank's equity investments would earn a return, as the bank would share in the profits of the business it financed.

The core strength of our nation's economy is rooted in fostering new industries and new technologies. Ironically, start-up capital is one of the most difficult forms of financing to obtain under our current financial system. We need to make it easier to start new companies. Financing new ventures would be a priority under Banking 2.0.

Let us look at how equity investments would work under Banking 2.0:

- Banks, as intermediaries of the Fed, would originate and service investments, making direct investments in equities as well as investing in PE funds, venture capital, and REITs. Banks would earn a percentage of the return from such investments and *pass the remainder to the Federal Reserve.* The Fed would

---

[35] Richards, R. D., *The Early History of Banking in England*, Routledge, 2012

serve as the bank's source of capital for investments and would set the investment criteria.[36]

• The Fed would *distribute the profits from its investments to our nation's citizens* in the form of Fed Dividends. Fed Dividends would *not* be considered government spending in calculating the rate for the FST; they would be a pass-through of profits, and as such they would represent justified growth in the money supply. The Fed would pass the profits from its equity investments to its beneficiaries—us!

THE TRUTH ABOUT INTEREST

The practice of banks charging interest can be traced back for thousands of years, and yet it is interesting to note how often interest has been prohibited and restricted. Among its critics have been Hinduism, Buddhism, Judaism, Christianity, and Islam. In addition, a number of philosophers, including Plato and Aristotle, condemned interest. Even Adam Smith, despite his

---

[36] The differentiating factor as to whether a financing is a loan or an investment would be based on whether the financing facilitates consumption or production. The purchase of a car or a home would be a loan, because buying a car or home is consumption. Financing a factory would be an investment, because factories generate production, warranting a return on the investment since the money supply must grow to correspond to the growth in the material economy that the factory generates.

advocacy of *laissez-fair* economics, supported limiting interest. [37]

I saw a curious problem with interest as a child. In school, we learned that compounding interest would continuously increase the value of an account over time. I saw that if one were to keep an account long enough, its balance would eventually grow to be equivalent to all the money in the world, no matter how small an amount of money one started with! The problem with this is that everyone else's money also earns interest. Thus the money supply itself must grow in order for all of us to earn interest, which means that the value of money must decline over time if interest is allowed.

It is common to think of the historical prohibitions against interest as being ideological in nature, not practical. I think, however, that the prohibitions against interest in the scriptures are practical, since interest erodes the value of money and degenerates the economy. It does not matter if it is an individual charging interest, a bank charging interest, or a government-issued Treasury bond earning interest; the effect on the economy is the same.

Today the use of interest is so commonplace that few consider it wrong. Even C. S. Lewis backed away from the issue in *Mere Christianity*,[38] writing:

---

[37] http://www.alastairmcintosh.com/articles/1998_usury.htm

[38] C. S. Lewis, *Mere Christianity*, Harper Collins, 1952

"There is one bit of advice given us by the ancient heathen Greeks, and by the Jews in the Old Testament, and by the Christian teachers of the Middle Ages, which the modern economic system has completely disobeyed. All these people told us not to lend money at interest. . . .That is a question I cannot decide on. I am not an economist and I simply do not know whether the investment system is responsible for the state we are in or not. . . .But I should not have been honest if I had not told you that three great civilizations had agreed. . . . in condemning the very thing on which we have based our whole life." (85)

I believe C. S. Lewis would have welcomed Banking 2.0, as it illustrates how the scriptures remain relevant today, even on the one subject he seemed uncertain of.

The last recession provided a prime example of how interest damages society. Remember bailing out the banks? We could have spent a lot less money, and experienced less carnage, had we required the banks to roll back interest rates on home loans.

Rolling back interest rates would have cut monthly payments for homeowners, which would have prevented foreclosures and stopped the slide in real estate values. The root cause of the recession was that the financial sector was costing us too much. By not addressing this problem, and by bailing out the banks instead, the financial sector ended up costing us even more. Our last recession would not have occurred under Banking 2.0.

The Key to Managing the Money Supply

Have you ever wondered why money has value? A good way to answer this question is to look at how gold has served as money over time. The notion that gold has value *in and of itself* has persisted for centuries, and this notion is part agreement, part illusion.

Historically, whenever we agreed that gold had value, it made it easier to transact business throughout the world. It might seem, therefore, that we can give value to money simply by agreeing that it has value—but that is an illusion.

There is an additional factor even more important than mutual agreement. In order for money to have value, *we must produce a corresponding value in the material economy*. In other words, we must produce goods and services. Otherwise, there is nothing to trade. With nothing to spend money *on*, money itself is valueless.

This was well illustrated during the California Gold Rush. As miners discovered gold, the money supply increased. Then, as more miners came to California, demand increased. The question soon became whether or not production could keep up with the growing money supply.

The answer, unfortunately, was no. Although venders rushed in to supply goods and services, the infrastructure for production was inadequate, and prices soared. Gold pans once worth 20 cents soon sold for $8, and the cost of an egg rose to $3, while eggs were only 2 cents elsewhere. That would be like paying $84 for an egg today.[39]

Nope. Not gold. Just a regular 'ol egg.

What we learn from this is that the value of gold is not merely a function of demand, or of how much gold there is; it is also a function of our ability to produce the

---

[39] http://www.ports.parks.ca.gov/pages/22922/files/Worksheet-GoldRushPrices.pdf.

goods and services gold is meant to buy. In other words, *money is only valuable if there is something to spend it on.*

Maintaining the value of money, therefore, is a two-fold task:

• We need to have an efficient and productive material economy that produces sufficient goods and services.

• We need to have a money supply in which there is sufficient money, but not too much.

If we are inefficient at producing goods and services, prices will go up. And even if we are efficient at producing goods and services, but we inflate our money supply, prices will go up.

The challenge today is that we lack the proper tools for managing the money supply. The Financial Settlements Tax and Banking 2.0 provide us with two of these tools, while Stimulus Payments, the subject of the next chapter, provides the remaining tool that we need. With these three tools, we can finally engineer our economy so that the monetary economy is working squarely to benefit *us*, the citizens of this nation.

"All money is a matter of belief."
—Adam Smith

CHAPTER FIVE

STIMULATING THE ECONOMY
More Money in Your Pocket

*"No complaint . . . is more common than
that of a scarcity of money."*
–Adam Smith

TAXING FINANCIAL SETTLEMENTS means more
than eliminating federal income taxes, balancing the
budget, and wiping out our nation's debt. The Financial
Settlements Tax opens the door to Stimulus Payments,
which are a means of augmenting our income, creating
jobs, and increasing production, all without inflating the
money supply.

The secret to increasing our prosperity lies in
understanding that our financial wherewithal depends
upon:

- Our ability to *produce* sufficient goods and
services, and

- Our ability to *buy* sufficient goods and services.

The Relationship between
Production and Consumption

The past few recessions demonstrate what happens when the capacity of consumers to buy falls below the capacity of our economy to produce. In the recession of 2008, for example, one of the main reasons that car manufacturers nearly went out of business was that there were not enough customers to purchase the vehicles they were making. Think about how you reacted to the recession. Did you buy fewer goods?

Recessions are characterized by a decline in consumption, sometimes even in nondurables like food.[40] In every recession, the health of the economy follows consumer spending.

> The best way to grow the economy is to ensure that the ability of consumers to purchase goods and services keeps up with the ability of businesses to produce.

Because of the extraordinary times we live in, the ability of businesses to produce is no longer the problem. Instead, the challenge is matching the ability of the consumer to buy with the ability of the producer to produce, which is why we need to capitalize growth.

---

[40] http://www.stanford.edu/group/recessiontrends/cgi-bin/web/sites/all/themes/barron/pdf/Consumption_fact_sheet.pdf

Capitalizing growth entails putting money in the hands of the consumer in the form of Stimulus Payments (SPs). If consumers are able to purchase more products, businesses will expand their production. For most companies today, profitability is primarily limited by the amount of customers they have (or do not have). When the biggest challenge that businesses face is having enough customers, the best thing we can do to improve our economy, and thus our standard of living, is to create more customers.

Take General Motors as an example. They could produce far more cars than they do today, but they lack sufficient demand. Suppose a delegation of government officials were to meet with General Motors and announce, "We have a problem. We've just completed a study, and the demand for cars is going to triple over the next three years. What can you do?" GM's management would not wring their hands—they would shout, "Hallelujah!"

The difference between the current level of production at GM, and the level that GM could produce if it had enough customers, defines the amount of *latent wealth* unrealized within GM. And it is the same for countless producers across the nation. We are sitting on a gold mine of latent wealth; we just need a means of tapping it.

Without a Financial Settlements Tax, there is no way to tap latent wealth. Today, if we wanted to inject cash into the economy, we would either have to increase taxes to remove that new money from the money supply or settle for inflation.

Under the program I am proposing, Stimulus Payments would entail distributing newly minted money to citizens in an amount sufficient to unlock our nation's latent wealth. In order to be sustainable, however, the distributed money would also have to be removed from the money supply with the FST, as illustrated in the below diagram.

If we remove the distributed money with the Financial Settlements Tax, it would enable us to stimulate the economy on a stable and continuous basis. The rate that our producers can tool up to meet the increased demand is thus the critical factor in determining the amount of money that should be distributed. If we distribute too much money, the price of goods will rise, and we will have done harm because demand will exceed supply. This is what happened during the California Gold Rush, as we saw in the previous chapter. If we distribute too little money, on the other hand, some latent wealth will remain unrealized.

The practical potential for Stimulus Payments was driven home for me a couple of years ago when I visited Kibera, the poor section of Nairobi, with a friend who had grown up there. There are no roads in that part of town, so you make your way on pathways between makeshift shacks.

Kibera turned out to be a thriving marketplace filled with entrepreneurs. There was only one thing missing, and that was cash. If everyone in Kibera had a few more shillings, the vendors would sell more goods, and they in turn could buy more goods. Even in third world nations, the ability to produce goods and services can exceed the ability of the people to buy goods and services. It is a classic "chicken and egg" problem that can be solved with Stimulus Payments.

I was so impressed with the potential for growth in Kibera that I turned to my friend and explained some of the fundamentals behind Stimulus Payments. "Do you think it would work in Kibera?" I asked. He smiled broadly and exclaimed, "Of course it would. These people want more: they just need the match to light the fire."

Since then I have looked into programs that are meant to pull people out of poverty. Generally they are weighted towards stimulating production instead of stimulating the ability of people to buy. Both sides of the equation are necessary. While it is true that without the ability to produce, more money will only inflate prices, it is also true that *without buyers, no one can afford to produce.* People are very inventive when the economic environment is conducive to making a profit. Give consumers money, and entrepreneurs will rise out of the dust to produce the goods and services that people need.

Variations of SPs have already been implemented where there is sufficient wealth for distribution. The State of Alaska voted to create the Alaska Department of Revenue's Permanent Fund Dividend Division, for example. As of 2013, the fund had over $49 billion in assets, and eligible citizens in Alaska have received dividends from the fund's profits for over thirty years.[41]

SPs also have precedence in oil-rich nations. Norway owns direct interests in the oil production that occurs on its continental shelf through an entity called the State's Direct Financial Interest (SDFI), which is managed by Petoro.[42] The income from SDFI provides 25% of the state's total income.[43] Norway utilizes some of the profits from SDFI to fund their Government Pension Fund and to provide tuition-free higher education for its citizens, as well as for foreign students.[44]

The key difference between such programs and the Stimulus Payments that I am proposing is that the former distributes *existing wealth*, whereas the latter *unlocks latent wealth*. Stimulus Payments, therefore, are a means for *increasing* our nation's wealth.

HOW THE MATH WORKS

Since Stimulus Payments are meant to stimulate consumer spending, it is reasonable to assume that a distribution weighted in favor of the poor and the middle

---

[41] For a record of the annual dividends paid and how the fund is administered visit http://www.apfc.org. If you are moving to Alaska, you can apply at: https://pfd.alaska.gov.

[42] http://www.petoro.no/home

[43] http://www.regjeringen.no

[44] http://www.timeshighereducation.co.uk/417752.article.

class would create more spending than a flat distribution. For the purposes of illustrating the power of SPs, however, we will take a conservative approach and calculate the effect based upon an even distribution to everyone.

Let us look at how much a Stimulus Payment would cost in terms of the Financial Settlement Tax. Assuming the population of the nation to be 315 million, each citizen could receive $3,174 from a distribution of $1 trillion. If the settlements being taxed total $4,456 trillion, a distribution of $1 trillion would increase the Financial Settlements Tax by 0.02%. In other words, the rate for the FST would increase from 0.1% to 0.12%.

> It would cost 20 cents in Financial Settlements Taxes per $1,000 in settlements to distribute $3,174 to everyone in the nation.

What would a Stimulus Payment of this size mean for a family of four earning $100,000? A distribution of $1 trillion would provide the family with an additional $12,696. And although the family's Financial Settlements Tax would increase by $35 because of the distribution, they would still come out ahead by $12,661.[45]

---

[45] Without the distribution of $1 trillion, the FST would be 0.1%, which equals $100 on earnings of $100,000. With a distribution of $1 trillion, the

While the Financial Settlements Tax eliminates the need for the IRS, Stimulus Payments mean that the people working at the IRS could keep their jobs. Instead of collecting revenue for the government, though, they would be sending revenue to us. Thus the Internal Revenue Service would be providing a *service*, sending us money, instead of taking our money.

Together the Financial Settlements Tax and Stimulus Payments would generate new prosperity for our nation. They represent upgrades to our operating system that facilitate real growth directly benefiting us. How we use this newfound wealth will be a testament to our heart.

"For where your treasure is, there your heart will be also."
–Jesus Christ, as quoted in Matthew 6:21 and Luke 12:34

FST would be 0.12%, which equals $135 on earnings of $112,696 (which is $100,000 plus 4 x $3,174; $1 trillion divided by a population of 315 million multiplied by four family members).

CHAPTER SIX

THE NEW AMERICAN DREAM
How the Solutions Come Together

Let us return to the characters introduced in the beginning of this book to see how the solutions I am proposing would combine to improve the lives of Americans of all economic levels.

TOM

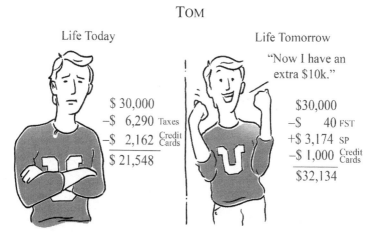

Life Today

$ 30,000
-$ 6,290 Taxes
-$ 2,162 Credit Cards
$ 21,548

Life Tomorrow

"Now I have an extra $10k."

$30,000
-$ 40 FST
+$ 3,174 SP
-$ 1,000 Credit Cards
$32,134

My solutions would net Tom over $10k in additional income each year. That represents a 49% improvement in Tom's discretionary income after he pays his obligations. Tom could afford to take courses at his local community college and launch his own online T-shirt business.

AMANDA

Life Today

$ 50,000
−$ 12,489 Taxes
−$ 4,578 Student Loan
−$ 5,405 Credit Cards
_____
$ 27,528

Life Tomorrow

"Now I have an extra 20k."

$50,000
- $ 64 FST
+$ 3,174 SP
- $ 2,500 Student Loan
- $ 2,500 Credit Cards
_____
$48,110

Today, it will take Amanda twenty years to pay off her debt, and she can barely afford $750 per month for an apartment. My solutions would boost Amanda's net disposable income by 74%, giving her an additional $20k annually. This would enable her to pay off her debt in four years, afford a home with a $400k mortgage, and still have $39k left over in disposable annual income.

JENNIFER AND JOE

Life Today		Life Tomorrow
		"Now we have an extra $57k."
$100,000		$100,000
–$ 22,574 Taxes		–$ 135 FST
–$ 25,764 Mtg		+$ 12,696 SP
–$ 9,156 Student Loan		–$ 13,333 Mtg
–$ 10,811 Credit Cards		–$ 5,000 Student Loan
$ 31,695		–$ 5,000 Credit Cards
		$ 89,228

Today, it will take Jennifer and Joe 20 years to pay off their debt, and they barely afford their $400k mortgage. My solutions would net Jennifer and Joe an additional $57k in disposable income—a 181% increase. This would enable them to pay off their debt in just 3 years, upgrade to a home with a $1 million mortgage, and still have $66k left over in annual disposable income.

The figures above were calculated from IRS tax tables and based upon certain assumptions.[46] Although

---

[46] Tom and Amanda's taxes were calculated as follows: income – $5,950 standard deduction – $3,800 personal exemption = value applied to tax table, plus income x .9235 x .133 per Form SE for Social Security tax. Jennifer and Joe's taxes were calculated as follows: gross income of $100,000 – $11,900 standard deduction – ($3,800 x 4 exemptions) = a tax of $10,291 based on the Form 1040 tax table, plus $100,000 x .9235 x .133 based on the Form SE for Social Security tax. No deduction was taken for mortgage interest, as it was assumed to be equal or less than the standard deduction. Credit card debt service for today was based upon an interest rate of 18% and a 10-year amortization. Credit card debt service for

the actual numbers will vary with everyone's circumstances, you can see how the solutions in this book would combine to substantially improve your finances.

Quite literally, the solutions I am proposing could net you twice the discretionary income that you have today. This is an astounding fact. It reflects just how great a burden the artificial barriers in our monetary economy are, and just how productive the material economy could be if we upgraded our operating system.

We need a monetary system that facilitates progress in our material economy rather than one that undermines productivity. Not only does our present operating system cost us too much money, it also has us riding a rollercoaster of booms and crashes.

When I was pitching my pool on Wall Street in the early '90's, it became apparent just how oblivious we can be about this rollercoaster ride. We were in the depths of a recession at the time, and I was meeting with a vice president of Prudential Securities. He predicted that my pool would never work, declaring, "Scott, real estate is dead. It's a new economy, and real estate will

---

Banking 2.0 was based upon an interest rate of 0% and a 10-year amortization. Student loan debt service for today was based upon an interest rate of 6.8% and a 20-year amortization. Student loan debt service for Banking 2.0 was based upon an interest rate of 0% and a 20-year amortization. Mortgage debt service for today was based upon an interest rate of 5% and a 30-year amortization. Mortgage debt service for Banking 2.0 was based upon an interest rate of 0% and a 30-year amortization.

never be what it once was. Investors will not buy debt backed by real estate."

A couple of years later the economy had turned around, and the rush to securitize mortgages was in full swing. Later in the '90's this same individual told me, "We are flying high, man! Real estate is sizzling. There's no end in sight!" The economy crashed shortly after that.

Contrast that to my grandfather's perspective. I was just starting to read the *Wall Street Journal* in the early '80's, and I was following the dire predictions of the pundits about the falling bond market. Then my grandfather surprised me by saying, "I just made my final investment decision in life. I sold everything and bought all 30-year Treasuries at 14%."

"Grandfather!" I exclaimed, alarmed that he could be so out of touch. "Haven't you heard there is no end in sight for climbing interest rates? If Treasuries hit 20% like they say, your bonds will be worthless!"

My grandfather laughed. "Oh, they always predict every boom and bust to last forever. Treasuries might go up a little more, but I don't care. You see, the market will always correct itself. An interest rate of 14% is simply not sustainable. Soon my bonds will command a premium price." And he was right.

I tell this story because it is important to recall our cycle of booms and busts; it provides a reality check for whatever the current thinking is on Wall Street. It could take a financial crisis to provide the jolt we need to enact the solutions I propose in this book.

When we are not in pain, it is easy to think that things will continue as they are. But eventually, *there will be a downturn.* And in the next downturn we may not be able to bail out the banks as we did in the last crisis—Banking 2.0 may be our only hope.

Together, the solutions I propose would give us the ability to self-direct our economy much as a conductor directs an orchestra. The Financial Settlements Tax is a valuable tool for managing the expansion and contraction of the money supply. Banking 2.0 allows us to set both the lending parameters and investment parameters that control economic activity in our nation. And Stimulus Payments provide a powerful tool to increase sales and production without inflation.

If, in fact, we adopt these solutions, we will need to make adjustments for our newfound economic power. For example, if banks no longer charge interest, housing prices will rapidly inflate unless the lending ratios for home mortgages are properly adjusted. By tightening lending ratios, we can keep home prices steady and make buying a home more affordable than it is today. This would have the added benefit of spurring an increase in consumer spending as well as creating more jobs.

We do not have comparable tools for managing our economy today. Consider how the Fed manages the money supply now, by adjusting interest rates: Bumping up interest rates increases the cost of production, as an element in the chain of production (finance) has been made more expensive. Manufacturers must thus either raise prices or live with smaller profit margins. Raising interest rates puts the brakes on the economy through disruptive financial friction, essentially crushing the economy. The image that comes to mind is the accordion effect in a train wreck.

Together, the tools I propose in this book provide us with a new economic dashboard for optimizing our nation's economy. We would finally have a financial system working squarely for the benefit of the American citizen.

OUR NEW ECONOMIC DASHBOARD

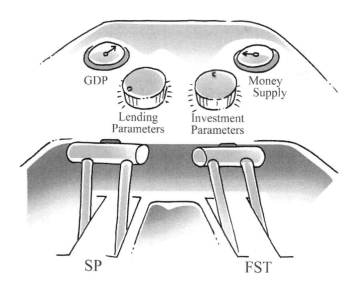

Indeed, if we implement these solutions, America's production engine would soon usher in a new era of wealth and prosperity. We stand at the brink of an opportunity that is unequaled in the history of our nation. The barriers before us are merely artificial constructs—ghosts of historical times gone by.

The solutions I am proposing are long overdue. The production engine in our material economy is primed and ready to provide the people of our nation with an unprecedented level of economic freedom and opportunity. We need only to make the changes I am proposing to set ourselves free.

"Three things cannot be long hidden:
the sun, the moon, and the truth."
–Buddha

Chapter Seven

Down-Home Economics

Modeling Tiny Economies—
Small Enough to Wrap Your Mind Around

In This Chapter I would like to give you a brief overview of how I arrived at the solutions I propose in this book. My search to understand the economy began at an early age, and one question in particular always bedeviled me. I would read in the newspaper about the ups and downs of the economy and wonder why this thing called the "economy" was so problematic to adults.

My intrigue deepened when I concluded that the economy was nothing more than "an accounting of our activities." Why would we choose to do well for a while and then choose to do badly? It did not make sense. One could understand hardships forced upon us, like famine and natural disasters, but self-inflicted ravages such as inflation, debt, and unemployment were maddening.

The concept of a nation striking it rich because it discovered gold did not fully pan out in my mind, either. What if a nation discovered gold *before* people had the ability to make goods? Cavemen must have stumbled upon some of the gold discovered in the California gold rush, for example, yet it would not have changed their lives. Similarly, the net worth of the world did not change when Spain found gold in the New World; the world's monetary system simply gave Spain a bigger slice of the pie.

At eight years old, I had the rare opportunity to travel around the world in an Airstream caravan.[47] During that 14-month trip, I was struck by the vast differences in lifestyles between people living in various countries. From that time on I was fascinated by economics and money. I asked myself questions like, "Why are some people poor and others rich? Why do some countries have roads while others use elephants? What is this mysterious thing called money, and why does it matter?"

---

[47] My family made the trip because my father landed a job as the writer to chronicle the journey. Back copies of his book, *Thank you, Marco Polo*, written in the 1960s, are still available on Ebay.

Much later in life, in order to better understand the problem, I decided to explore the notion of the *material economy* as compared to the *monetary economy*. Think of the material economy as the actions of people and their machines, especially with regard to production and consumption. Think of the monetary economy as the movement of money, as described by the economic indicators reported in the *Wall Street Journal*.

The material economy is what you could discern about a civilization if you were to view it through a telescope. As an avid amateur astronomer in my early years, I used to imagine this all the time. If you could see that the citizens of a particular civilization have their own flying machines, live in luxurious homes, enjoy communications with anyone in their solar system, and are serviced by robots that manufacture everything, you could conclude that their economy is more efficient than ours. You would not need to know anything about their "economic indicators" to make this assessment.

Furthermore, if you were to obtain news feeds from the civilization and find that their monetary system is in shambles, their planetary debt is mounting, and their version of a stock market had lost fifty percent of its value in the last year, you would search for the root of the problem in their material economy. Perhaps they are running out of a key natural resource and their lifestyle is in peril. Absent such a reason, however, you would conclude that their monetary system is somehow out of sync with their material economy.

I wondered whether our nation might not be in a similar situation. Ever since I was a child, my father had been predicting the demise of our monetary system. Yet despite our mounting national debt and a plethora of alarming monetary-based indicators, it seemed to me that our material economy was improving, as we did not have the Internet or smart phones when I was a child.

And so I wondered, what if it our monetary economy is simply out of sync with our material economy? What if our monetary economy is working against our material economy, and there is something we can do about it?

These are provocative questions, to be sure. My heart skipped a beat when I first thought of them. I was fascinated with the impact that securitization was having on the economy, and I sensed there was more we could do to increase efficiency in the monetary system. I wanted to understand how our economic problems would play out when explored from a monetary and a material perspective. I needed to gain a better perspective on the problem; it was time to reduce complicated issues to simple models. I decided to model tiny economies that were small enough to wrap my mind around.

The economies I modeled only have a few people, but they clearly illustrate the basis of our economic problems, and they suggest solutions. They are similar to the diagrams a football coach draws on a marker board. I have always liked the "X's" and "O's" with arrows that coaches draw showing what the players are supposed to do on the field. Those diagrams are simple, reducing a myriad of variables to simple patterns that make sense. They also provide a basis for analyzing a play and how to improve it in the future. That is the way I approached my analysis of our economy, and it is how we will approach economic modeling in this chapter.

MODELING THE ECONOMY

Let us begin our quest by creating a material economy with just three people: a farmer and hunter who produce food, and a handyman who produces clothing, housing, and tools. Since we will need a benchmark to model various scenarios against, let us start with the assumption that all three members of the economy work eight hours per day, five days per week, and produce just enough for each member to have what they need. From this benchmark we will be able to explore various economic scenarios, starting with a tiny economy that does not use money, and then later introducing the use of money.

The Economic Impact of Decreased Productivity

In the next three scenarios, we will explore the effect that declines in *production* and *productive efficiency* have on the material economy. You will see that these scenarios put a rather interesting spin on the concept of inflation.

Scenario 1
A Decline in Productive Efficiency

Let us consider the ramifications if the farmer has to work twice the hours—16 hours per day, 5 days per week—to produce the same amount of food. Let us also presume that the same amount of goods change hands between the three members of society.

From the farmer's perspective, he is experiencing a loss in his trading power. This is like inflation to him, since he now has to work twice as hard to buy the same amount of goods and services, including the farm produce he grows for himself. From the hunter and handyman's perspective, there has been no change in their buying power. Thus, from the perspective of the material economy:

- Inflation is a decline in one's ability to acquire goods relative to the amount of time one works.

- Inflation will result from a decline in one's productive efficiency.

SCENARIO 2
A Decline in Productive Output

Now let us contrast the previous scenario with what happens when the farmer's productive efficiency is halved, but he does *not* increase the hours that he works—instead he continues to work 8 hours per day, 5 days per week. He thus produces half as many crops. Let us also presume that the production of the hunter and the handyman remain the same, and everyone exchanges a third of their production for a third of the others' production.

From everyone's perspective, they are experiencing inflation in terms of the cost of farm goods, as they are each receiving half as much farm produce per hour they work.

From this scenario, we can conclude:

• If per capita production drops, we all become poorer.

• Inflation can result from a drop in the productive efficiency or productive output of a few.

This is the basis behind the notion that "everyone must pull their weight or suffer the consequences." In this scenario, the effect of decreased production on the part of one member of society clearly affects the other members.

SCENARIO 3
Limiting the Impact of a Decline in Output

Once again we will halve the farmer's productivity yet retain his normal hours so that he produces half as much as he did in the benchmark economy. This time, however, let us see if the impact of the decline in the farmer's output can be handled so it only affects the farmer, not the handyman or the hunter.

The only way to accomplish this would be for the farmer to receive a disproportionately smaller amount of his production. That way, in theory, the others would not suffer a loss. There is a limit to which this strategy will work, however. In our scenario, there would *not* be enough for the handyman and hunter to receive their benchmark standard of farm produce, even if the farmer keeps nothing for himself.

The meaning of this scenario is straightforward. If the drop in production is significant enough, a few members of society cannot be made poor enough to prevent the remaining members from suffering losses. In fact, this is exactly what happens when the economy takes a tumble: consumer spending declines, and sales slow. Because sales slow, producers have to cut back on production and lay off workers, fueling a vicious cycle. Everyone loses.

INCREASED PRODUCTIVITY AND NEW WEALTH

In the next two scenarios, we will look at the effect of increased production on the economy.

SCENARIO 4
An Increase in Productive Efficiency and Output

In this scenario, the handyman invents a plow, allowing the farmer to double his production. In addition, the farmer learns to raise animals, providing the village with twice as many animals as the hunter can, so the hunter retires. Upon seeing how the plow improves the farmer's productivity, the handyman invents tools for himself as well, doubling his own production.

In the meantime, the hunter marries, and the couple has twin daughters—now there are six members in our tiny economy. With the farmer's and handyman's newfound productivity, there is plenty for everyone without the hunter or his family having to work.

Early in the industrial age, many argued against replacing hand labor with efficient factories, claiming that society could not withstand the hit on employment. This scenario, however, shows that a sufficient increase in the productivity of some can lessen the workload of others, and no one has to suffer a loss in their standard of living.

This may seem unfair if we believe that everyone must pull their own weight, or others will suffer. While this dictum holds true when productivity drops below a certain point, *it is not true when productivity exceeds a certain point.* Instead, the opposite is true—if there is no one to consume, the extra production has no value, and there is no reason to overproduce.

Once productive efficiency reaches a certain level, therefore, the wealth of our nation, as well as the profitability of its producers, is limited by whether or not there are enough customers to buy the producers' goods. This has nothing to do with whether or not the customers are producing anything. While we must reward production, as the producers are "the geese that lay the golden eggs," we must also enable consumption; otherwise production will diminish in value.

These scenarios led me to the idea of Stimulus Payments, which encourage consumption by increasing the buying power of customers. I saw that our American economy possessed remarkable productive power. Our problem was not a lack of production but rather surplus. Thus SP's are increasingly necessary as we become more efficient at producing.

SCENARIO 5
Increased Efficiency and Output Lead to New Jobs

Let us explore the concept of increased efficiency further. In the previous scenario, the handyman and the farmer had increased their production by utilizing advancements in technology, and the two were providing for a village of six. The hunter and his wife, along with their two daughters, were the beneficiaries of this new efficiency, enjoying the excess production without having to work.

Historically, however, as technology has replaced jobs, workers have engaged in new activities, further improving our standard of living. Modeling this is simple: the hunter modifies his weapons to protect the village against invaders. Then he sets about building footpaths to make it easier to enter the forest and gather raw materials. He also founds a school, chronicling what he has discovered about the natural world. The hunter's wife learns to cook and prepares sumptuous feasts for the village, while the daughters become musicians and dancers, providing entertainment after dinner.

The quality of life within the village is thus improved. Now the members of the village not only have enough food, clothing, and shelter, but they also enjoy increased security, better transportation, improved knowledge, culinary delights, and entertainment. Historically, when our necessities are provided for, we pursue leisure activities, luxury goods, and entertainment.

Had the farmer and handyman refused to share the products of their labor with the hunter and his family, the family would never have been able to develop their new skills, and the wealth of the village would not have been increased. This scenario further illustrates the value of Stimulus Payments. Based on this scenario, we can conclude that:

• Distributing wealth spawns even more producers, whose production further enriches society, meeting needs that were previously unknown.

INTRODUCING GOVERNMENT INTO THE ECONOMY

In the previous scenario, we assigned to the hunter activities that are typically roles for the government: protecting society from outside attack, building roads, and creating schools. On the other hand, we are not likely to consider the activities that the hunter's wife and daughters engaged in—cooking meals and dancing—as governmental activities.

What really differentiates the government from the private sector, though, apart from our conventional biases? After all, building roads and schools can certainly be accomplished under the auspices of the private sector, while there are numerous examples of government-sponsored art.

It is not the nature of the activity, but rather the fact that we vest authority in the government that determines whether something is public or private. It is the authority of the government, for example, that makes schools "public." There is nothing inherent about schools that require them to be public. The same is true for any other activity. In the next two scenarios, therefore, we will examine the concepts of government and governmental spending from the perspective of the material economy.

The Origins of Government and Spending

We return to the tiny economy in which the farmer and handyman have become productive enough to fully provide for themselves, as well as for the hunter and his family. This time, however, because of the hunter's physical strength and prowess with weapons, he establishes his authority as the village chief. He creates rules for others to follow, enforces them when broken, and plans for the fortification of the village.

If the village is threatened, the village chief presses the farmer and handyman into service and leads them in battle. He busies himself with building fortifications for the village, pressing the others into duty when he needs their labor. From this we see that:

• "Government" is the authority to execute projects that consume a state's resources and regulate the activities of its citizens.

SCENARIO 7
The Material Economy Cannot Have a Deficit

When the village chief presses the farmer and handyman into duty to help build fortifications for the village, the task requires a certain amount of labor and natural resources. If the task exceeds what the village can afford, *the task is impossible to complete.* In other words, if the village wall requires 100 fence posts, but the villagers only have 50 fence posts, the wall cannot be completed. From a material perspective, therefore, the government can never "spend" more than it can afford.

This conclusion surprised me, leading to years of trying to unravel the ramifications for our own government's deficit. When I first began exploring this scenario, my goal had been to establish, from the perspective of the material economy, what it means for the government to run a deficit. But by examining spending from the perspective of the material economy, I made the surprising discovery that:

• The government's deficit cannot be modeled in the material economy, as a deficit in the material economy is simply not possible.

Once this was clear, it became evident that there must be a way to resolve our nation's deficit and repay our national debt. If the concept of a deficit is *nonexistent* in the material economy, then a deficit *must* be a construct of the monetary economy. Therefore, it must always be possible to eliminate a deficit with the right adjustments to the monetary system.

When observed from a material perspective, the checks and balances on what society can and cannot accomplish are set by physical reality and cannot be violated. In this regard, a government can never "borrow from the future." And indeed, we will never find ourselves transporting people or resources into the past to make up for "deficit spending."

Our deficit is a construct of the monetary system we have adopted. In reality, we are able to pay for everything we do; otherwise we would run short of resources before the projects were complete.

So, if we are able to afford all we are doing as a nation, how have we ended up with a deficit? The answer is found in the monetary system, which is the subject of the next five scenarios.

Scenario 8
Adding Money to the Material Economy

To explore the effects of money in our tiny economy, let us return to the original benchmark scenario, in which the farmer, handyman, and hunter all perform a full day's work, providing each other with just enough to meet their needs. If our villagers choose gold as their form of money, and have none, they will be left staring at each other at the end of a hard day of labor, wondering how they are going to afford one another's goods. Silly—yet it illustrates the fundamental problems that Stimulus Payments and Banking 2.0 solve.

Let us consider what happens if the farmer finds some gold and runs back to the village with the good news that they can finally buy one another's goods. How can trade begin if the farmer has all the gold? He must start the purchasing chain by paying the handyman and the hunter one nugget of gold each, thus buying a third of the goods they have produced. That way, the handyman and hunter will be able to swap nuggets, purchasing a third of each other's production. Finally, the handyman and hunter will each pay the farmer a nugget of gold for a third of his produce, and the transaction will have come full circle. Now, in this case, our three friends do not need money at all; they could just swap goods. But for the sake of illustrating the way money complicates the economy, we will force them to use gold to buy one another's products.

If they continue this cycle, all will be well. But if they alter the order of exchange at all—if the handyman and hunter choose to buy farm produce *before* purchasing one another's produce—they will be faced with a problem. They will have no nuggets left to buy each other's produce, simply because they shopped in the wrong order.

Our tiny economy will have encountered a crisis precipitated by a flaw in its monetary system, which would be a shame because the problem would be artificial and would not reflect a real issue in their material economy. Likewise, the economic problems we face today are artificial constructs of our monetary economy and do not reflect any real issues in the material economy—yet if left unresolved, they will continue to negatively impact the material economy. The truth is, a liquidity crisis in our economy is just as laughable as the liquidity crisis I described in the above paragraph.

Even if the villagers follow the appropriate protocol, making exchanges in the correct order, their material economy will be cumbersome because of their monetary system. Let us consider some solutions to facilitate the handyman and hunter's ability to make timely exchanges, without having to wait on gold from the farmer. One solution is for them to find their own gold. That would free them to purchase goods from each other as soon as goods are available for sale.

Another solution is for the farmer to distribute gold to the handyman and hunter so they will each have enough to make purchases whenever goods are available. We can see, based on this example, just how bankers achieved such power as aggregators of money.

It is also apparent that if the farmer were to lend the handyman and hunter gold and charge interest for it, a crisis would occur once their gold reserves ran dry. In fact, the problem with charging interest becomes evident whenever modeling tiny economies. Interest absorbs money from the economy, and unless the money supply is inflated, trade is inevitably compromised. Thus we see the need for Banking 2.0.

Why would the farmer be willing to distribute gold to the handyman and hunter? Well, keeping the gold does not make him any wealthier, since his material wealth is limited by the daily production of the village. In fact, the wealth of the village has nothing to do with the amount of gold the villagers have. Thus we see that:

- Money is only a "permission slip" to receive material goods and services.

- The true wealth of a nation is determined by the amount of goods and services that the nation produces, not by the amount of money it creates.

Scenario 9
Expanding the Money Supply

Let us explore what happens if the villagers have an overabundance of gold. Obviously, their purchasing power is limited by their production. They cannot buy more food than the farmer grows or more tools than the handyman builds. So excess money will do nothing to increase their material wealth. A problem will arise, however, if one of the villagers over-spends. If, for example, the hunter buys two thirds of the farmer's produce one day because he has the gold to do so, the handyman will have to go without vegetables.

An abundance of gold would also permit the villagers to bid up the price of goods or overprice the goods they are selling. This would be an example of monetary inflation, which is distinct from the form of inflation we explored at the beginning of this chapter, in which one's buying power is eroded due to a drop in productive efficiency.

If the buyer's supply of money is growing at the same rate that prices are increasing, simply because the supply of money has increased (a large find of gold has flooded the market, perhaps), then the buyer's purchasing power remains unaffected, and it is irrelevant that the face value of prices have increased. The end value of the permission slips has not changed.

An abundance of money will not necessarily cause monetary inflation. Monetary inflation requires the volition of the members of society, as people may choose to conserve their cash rather than spend it. If, in fact, gold is so abundant that the villagers set the price for a day's supply of goods at three nuggets of gold instead of one, there is no harm in it. The greater harm is when there is a lack of money, and there are goods available for purchase but no means to buy them.

SCENARIO 10
Taxation

Having introduced money into our tiny economy, let us examine how money affects the government. In this scenario the farmer and handyman are again productive enough to fully provide for themselves, as well as for the hunter. As before, because of the hunter's physical strength and prowess with weapons, he establishes his authority as the village chief, creating rules that the others must follow.

This time, however, the chief extends his authority to taxing the villagers. Let us assume that everyone has found sufficient gold and that they have long been exchanging nuggets for goods and services.

If the chief decides that the village needs fortifying, he has a choice. He could require the farmer and handyman to help him with the project, or he could decide to pay for their help. Governments have faced this choice throughout history. Some governments have pressed people into service, while others have paid for labor.

We know from the perspective of the material economy that the chief can never undertake a project that results in a deficit, since a project more ambitious than his village can afford cannot be completed. Because the village now has a monetary economy, and the chief needs a source of gold to pay for the project, he must either tax the villagers or come up with the gold himself.

Whether the chief can *pay* for the project or not is simply a function of the amount of gold he has access to, a factor that is independent of the villagers' ability to complete the project. If, in fact, the chief cannot pay for the project, even though the village can complete it, it would be analogous to the scenario in which the villagers had produced the goods and services they needed, but were unable to purchase them from each other. This is an important lesson, as it shows that:

- The ability of a government to collect sufficient money to pay for projects is unrelated to the ability of a nation to accomplish the project, but is instead dependent upon the government's ability to access sufficient money in a way that does not negatively impact trade.

SCENARIO 11
A Balanced Budget

Let us suppose the farmer and handyman have become so efficient at their jobs that they are only working half a day, but the village chief is working overtime to fortify the village. When the chief solicits the farmer and handyman's help, they each demand three nuggets of gold per day for their labor. Their rationale is that they already receive two nuggets of gold for a half day of labor, in addition to keeping one third of their production, so if they are going to work another half day they should receive three nuggets of gold for their work. It makes sense from a monetary point of view, so the chief agrees.

In order to have a balanced budget, the chief needs to collect four nuggets daily from both the farmer and the handyman: one from each of them to buy their goods, and three from each of them to cover their labor on the fortification of the village. If the villagers have sufficient gold, and agree on this plan, they have a government with a balanced budget.

Deficit Spending

Because the village's monetary system is independent of its material economy, it has the potential to needlessly complicate itself. It is easy to propose a scenario in which the village government incurs a deficit, even though the villagers have sufficient monetary resources to balance their budget.

Let us suppose that the farmer and handyman are outraged by the chief's proposal that he increase taxes by three nuggets per day to pay for their labor, as they see his proposal as a circular scheme in which they are really just paying themselves. If the chief defers to their objection and agrees to pay the farmer and handyman for their labor from his own reserve, he will be operating on a deficit of six nuggets per day, and it will only be a matter of time before he runs out of money.

Once the chief's reserves are exhausted, he might be tempted to borrow from the farmer and the handyman, since their reserves would be flush with gold. His debt would have the potential to grow indefinitely, especially if the farmer and handyman charged him interest.

Although this scenario illustrates a monetary economy in a dismal predicament, it is apparent that the problem is artificial and can be remedied. We see that the problem does not rest with the villagers' actual ability to fortify their village, but merely with a flaw in their monetary system. It is the same for our government today, and it was this analysis that gave me the basis for the economic solutions that I have proposed in this book.

Scenarios 8-12 illustrate the simple fact that, while money is useful for facilitating trade, it can also complicate things.

• Introducing money into the economy allows the possibility of a divided economy, in which the monetary economy works against the material economy and creates an unnecessary deficit.

In the end, these twelve scenarios confirmed my initial hunch. There is nothing wrong with our nation's production engine; it has merely been stifled by artificial financial constructs such as income taxes, a financial deficit, skyrocketing debt, and interest.

As in the above scenario, our monetary economy is simply out of synch with our material economy. The good news is that there is something we can do about it. Once we grasp that the monetary economy is a synthetic construct whose only real purpose is to facilitate growth in the material economy, it is possible to develop solutions like the Financial Settlements Tax, Coupon Stripping, Stimulus Payments, and Banking 2.0.

In the next chapter, I describe my personal journey so you can know a little about me and what motivates me to seek the changes I am advocating.

CHAPTER EIGHT

MY JOURNEY
The Long and Winding Road

WALKING DOWN MAIDEN Lane in lower Manhattan over twenty years ago, I felt like an inconspicuous speck on the street. I remember looking around and thinking, "Wow, this is what it means to feel small." I was an outsider to Wall Street. Everyone was so well dressed, and I was not. The investment bankers had classy educations from Ivy League schools, and I did not. They were rolling in money, and I was not.

I had been making trips to Wall Street for two years by then and was still trying to put the same deal together. It was tough going, and I was beginning to think my dream of selling bonds on Wall Street to fund loans was not going to work. The Savings & Loan crisis was in full swing, and millions of property owners were scrambling just to keep their heads above water. The banks were under instruction not to renew commercial mortgages, so if your mortgage was maturing, you were out of luck.

We had just moved to Colorado when the crisis hit, and the bank that had hired me closed its doors on my second day on the job. I remember the bank manager saying, "I hope you didn't move out here just for this job." I had. Fortunately I landed a job at a second bank, but it closed two weeks later. I was hired at yet a third bank, but it closed in two months.

There was a lot of finger pointing when the Savings and Loan crisis hit, with everyone casting blame from their own perspective. Politicians were out for their pound of flesh, but meanwhile, real people were suffering. I was focused on my own problem, of course, which was, "How do I earn a living in this recession?"

I turned to an idea I had been mulling over before moving to Colorado. I decided to put together my own pool of mortgages and take it to Wall Street for financing. My plan was to have investment bankers sell bonds to raise the capital necessary to finance all the mortgages. We would then combine the monthly payments of the mortgages to repay the bonds over time. I had developed a way of prioritizing the mortgage payments so that the bonds would have various levels of risk and return, thus appealing to a variety of investors.

The plan turned out to be a good one, but looking back on my goal, I realize how impossible it should have seemed. I was convinced it could be done, though—and besides, I had no idea how else to earn a living considering the state of the economy.

I did not know a soul on Wall Street before making my first trip to New York. I knew no one at the rating agencies. And I had only $425 to start my company. But I believed that the structure I had conceived would work, so I doggedly set out to accomplish the impossible.

It helped that everyone was desperate for financing. Today, I tell people that if you had climbed the highest peak in Colorado back then and merely whispered, "I think I may have a source for money," a crowd would have gathered. When we announced we were seeking borrowers for a mortgage pool, we were besieged with applicants.

My conversations with the would-be borrowers were brutal:

"Have you ever done this before?" they would ask.

"No one has," I would answer.

"What guarantee can you give me that this will work?" they would want to know.

"Absolutely none," I would say. Then I would conclude, "Look, if you have any other option at all, take it. If you have absolutely no other option, you might consider taking a chance on our pool."

The devastation in that recession was so great that we had no lack of borrowers. They came from all walks of life. Once proud high-flyers who used to wine and dine with elite bankers were now scrambling. Small-time owners who used to shake hands with their neighborhood banker to close a deal now had to call on out-of-state strangers. It seemed that the very fabric of our country was coming apart. And in large measure it was, just as it does in every recession.

It was hard to get appointments with the investment banks at first. Their reactions varied. To be sure, there were some sympathizers. But even to them, my proposal seemed far-fetched. At first there were far more detractors than there were supporters. Some were outright hostile: I was read the riot act more than once, escorted out of offices, and humiliated. It was hard to continue when that happened; I would wonder if I was fooling myself.

Little by little, we made progress. Eventually, I was invited to speak at a conference. I remember looking across the sea of pin-stripped suits and wondering if I would be asked questions that I could not answer. I wondered if I would be found out—exposed as just another nobody.

My talk went fairly well at first. People had lots of questions, and they were mostly enthusiastic. Then someone asked me a pointed question: "You've been at this for some time now. If this is such a good idea, why haven't you been able to close?" He was one of the ones who had kicked me out of his office. I had been going to Wall Street for two years by then and still had no takers.

My answer was to the point. "It will happen when someone finally steps up and funds the pool. It's a new idea, so it's taken time for people to accept. But once funded, the pool will work, the bonds will sell, and the investors will be happy."

Then someone asked what I thought the size of the market was. I was surprised, thinking to myself, "Isn't it obvious?" I gamely offered, "Look, there's a dearth of money for lending today. There are hundreds of billions of dollars in commercial real estate loans that need refinancing. The size of the market is the amount of commercial real estate debt in our nation."

In the end, the size of the market surprised even me. The market not only included all the commercial real estate debt in our nation, but also residential real estate debt, car and equipment loans, credit card receivables, and more. In all, tens of trillions of dollars of debt were securitized in the years that followed. This led to my understanding of the power behind financial technologies—just as computer technologies, transportation technologies, and energy technologies fuel the economy, so do financial technologies. That understanding became the basis for the solutions I propose in this book.

A couple of months after the conference, the investment bank DLJ expressed an interest in the pool. After weeks of due diligence, it finally came down to a committee vote. I remember staying late in the office with Jerry Verbeck, who is still my business partner today, contemplating everything we had sent to DLJ and wondering if there was anything else we could have said or done. Now the decision of whether or not to proceed with the pool was up to someone else. Our fate would be decided the next day, and there was nothing more we could do. Jerry summed it up: "Tomorrow we will either be heroes or scoundrels; it could go either way."

The next day DLJ agreed to finance the pool. The only caveat was that I would have to find the buyer for the unrated bonds—the most risky portion of the mortgage pool. I agreed, as we had no alternative. Surely one of our borrowers could come up with the money, I thought.

But I could find no buyers. I grew increasingly anxious because DLJ was proceeding with the project, apparently confident we could sell the unrated bonds. You would think they would have questioned me daily about how it was going, but they did not.

We had sixty days to come up with a buyer, so I pitched everyone I could find, but to no avail. As the deadline loomed, I flew to New York for a last-ditch meeting with the final prospect. The meeting was in the World Trade Center, and the outcome was a quick "No."

I walked out to the busy sidewalk after the meeting, thinking, "So this is how it all ends." I wondered if I should call the office and let my employees go first, or call DLJ. In that moment I surrendered, giving up for the first time in my life. It was an important spiritual lesson for me, as I have a hard time letting go.

As I stood on the sidewalk, numb and thinking there was nothing more I could do, someone walked up and said, "Aren't you Scott Smith?" He introduced himself as being with Daiwa, the huge Japanese bank, and said he had met me at the conference after my speech. He remembered that I was from Colorado and asked what I was doing in New York.

"Selling the B-bonds," I said.

He looked at me incredulously. "For the same pool you were showing at the conference?" he asked.

"Yes," I said, worried he would express shock that the pool still had not closed.

"How amazing I've run into you," he exclaimed. "Just this morning Andy Stone announced that Daiwa was in the market for high-yield paper. Can you imagine what a hero I'd be if I delivered B-bonds an hour later? Can we buy them?"

"Sure," I stammered. Daiwa was located in the World Finance Center, right across from the World Trade Center, so we crossed the street. A couple of hours later I was in my hotel room on the phone with DLJ, telling them in a matter-of-fact tone that we had sold the B-bonds to Daiwa. When I called my office in Boulder, I was anything but matter-of-fact!

My elation soon turned to despair, however. We had two weeks to complete the paperwork, and in the final days Mr. Stone began re-trading. At first I thought he was positioning for a better price, but the night before the deadline he announced, "I'm not doing the deal" and hung up.

I remember thinking, "It was improbable to come across a buyer on the sidewalks of New York, but no one is going to knock on my door late at night in Boulder; this deal is dead." I surrendered again, giving up all hope. I would have to level with DLJ in the morning.

When I walked into the office the next morning, the phone was ringing. It was Larry Brown, the attorney for DLJ. He was bubbling with excitement. "Call us crazy, but at this morning's meeting Jim Roiter asked, 'Why are we letting Andy Stone buy the B-bonds? Get on the phone and see if it's too late for us to buy them!' And so I'm on the phone. Is it too late?"

"No, it's not too late. You can have them," I said, somewhat breathless. A couple of weeks later we were closing loans. It seemed almost anticlimactic.

Once the deal began to move forward, however, everything turned hectic. One of the biggest challenges was the lack of protocol, as mortgage conduits were such a new idea. An illustration of this occurred a few months into the transaction. I received an alarmed call from Larry, who said, "Jim and I are on the next plane to Colorado! The guys upstairs discovered we haven't signed any paperwork with you, and we've been wiring you millions of dollars. You could walk away with the loans you've closed, and there's nothing we could do!"

The next day the three of us were typing up a document from scratch. They decided to create a line of credit. DLJ would lend us the money for each mortgage we closed, and we would deliver the loan to them as security. When the pool closed, it would pay off the line of credit. Watching them typing, I thought, "Is this really how they do things on Wall Street?"

The subject of how large the line of credit should be came up. "How many loans do you have?" they asked.

"$200 million and counting," I replied.

They thought about it. Jim said, "We want his next pool, too, you know."

Larry said, "How about $500 million, then?"

Jim said, "His next pool is going to be bigger. Make it a billion dollars."

As I drove home that night, I thought about how rapidly my life had changed. Not long ago I had feared all would crash and burn, and now we had a billion dollar line of credit. The pool turned out to be more than a success for our company—the structure helped transform the financial world. It initiated what became known as "conduit financing," and within a few months every investment bank on Wall Street had a conduit program.

Securitization was a powerful vehicle for financing real estate. It precipitated years of unprecedented growth for our economy. In fact, the economy did so well that, for two years of Clinton's administration, our nation did not have a deficit. Securitization also served to dramatically reduce mortgage interest rates, which made home ownership much more affordable.

Years later, securitization was abused through the use of credit default swaps. Credit default swaps are simply promises made by insurers to make good on bonds backed by mortgages, should the mortgages go into default. Notably, credit default swaps were not part of the structure I had promoted. I intended each pool to have its own cash reserve to cover defaults, which is the way it should be.

With our first pool, DLJ called and asked me to check the cost of insuring the bonds. They were hoping that the ratings could be improved if the bonds were insured. I looked into it and found that credit default swaps did not make sense, as we had already self-insured the pool with a cash reserve.

I called DLJ back and said, "Insuring the bonds doesn't make sense. The cash reserve reflects the risk of the pool. Insuring the bonds would cost the same as the reserve, *plus* overhead and profit for the insurer."

Tragically, credit default swaps resurfaced years later because insurers agreed to premiums priced at a fraction of what they should have been. The latest financial crisis would not have occurred if Wall Street had continued to use properly-funded cash reserves instead of relying on credit default swaps to finance mortgage pools.

You would think I would have been home free after landing a billion-dollar line of credit, but a few months later I was in the doctor's office receiving the news that I had a brain tumor. That tumor changed my life as rapidly as the line of credit had. It put me in a tailspin that was not good for business, and the years that followed were humbling. As my health worsened, my company faltered, and I became despondent. DLJ took over the pool, but they gave us the right to continue sending loans to them. They were kind. It was a challenging time in so many respects. I know what it means to feel that you would be better off dead than alive.

Today I look back and see that my trials were good for me—they taught me humility. If it had been smooth sailing, and I had made a killing on Wall Street, it would have been destructive for me personally. Most of the owners of commercial real estate we worked with had broken lives. Their wealth brought them no happiness. I thought I was immune to their challenges; I thought I would handle it differently. Today I know that I would not have.

As is so often the case in life, the challenges that I faced brought about new opportunities. It was during this time that we became involved in the first phase of Nelson Mandela's Redevelopment Project (RDP) in South Africa, which provided housing for 11,000 families near Soweto. I never visited the project, and today I wish I had. The photos were amazing. In the midst of personal challenges, it was nice to see the smiling faces of families building their first home. It gave me a sense of hope.

We experienced an interesting coincidence while helping with the RDP financing. The amount of money Mandela needed for 11,000 houses was $5 million. At the same time a mortgage broker forwarded us a loan request from Donald Trump, also for $5 million, for refinancing one of Trump's personal residences in Manhattan. The irony that both financings required the same amount of money was not lost on us.

It was easy to find Trump the financing he wanted, though he turned us down because our interest rate was too high. It took years to put the deal together in South Africa, and they probably would have accepted whatever interest rate we could find. I'm happy to say we provided our services gratis. The loan officer who shepherded the transaction later left the financial field to become a church leader.

It was also during this time that I started Kidz Magazine with a friend, Glenn Meyers. We had no idea what we were doing, which is why the magazine's tagline was "By kids, for kids."

Our idea for the magazine was simple enough: let the kids write all the content and create all the art. The inspiration for the magazine came from some time I spent volunteering in the classroom. The students never liked their reading and writing assignments, but they sure enjoyed talking to each other. I figured, if you let them write what they want, they would enjoy reading the magazine—and they did.

Kidz Magazine was distributed through schools, with teachers handing it out in the classroom. It was free to schools because we sold advertising to pay for the cost of printing. Over the years it grew, spreading from city to city. Eventually it spanned over 30 nations, with millions of readers.

After the tumor was diagnosed, I began running the trails around Boulder. Running made me feel better. When I was outside in nature, I could forget my problems for a while. As I ran, I would fall into a near sleep state. I can remember the trees sliding by effortlessly, and the peace I would feel. Once again I was surrendering, and it was another step in the right direction, just as my experience outside the World Trade Center had been.

One day as I was running, more than two years after the tumor was diagnosed, I experienced something very startling. Out of nowhere I heard a voice say, "You're well now." It was so distinct. At the time I did not believe in God and had no idea what to make of what I had heard. But the voice spoke with such authority I was compelled to call my doctor to schedule an MRI.

The doctor was able to see me the next morning, and he called me that night with the results. "You don't have a tumor anymore," he said. He explained that he had never seen a tumor spontaneously disappear like that, but he had heard of it happening.

With my new lease on life I was inspired to try new endeavors, so I committed to co-founding two charter schools. It was a controversial undertaking that offended the status quo in the school district. At the end of my daughter's fifth grade year, I remember a teacher making her sit alone in the corner of the classroom and read while the rest of her classmates enjoyed a pizza party. The reason? Layla had elected to attend the charter school I had co-founded, while the other students had decided to attend their neighborhood middle school. The pizza party was only for those going to the school that the district approved of.

Both charter schools were great successes in the end, but it was a long and challenging road to launch them. Every week we spent countless hours working until late at night. The school district fought us tooth and nail on both schools. They felt they had made a mistake in giving us a facility for the first school—Summit Middle School—so they required us to find our own site for the second school, Peak-to-Peak.

Finding a site took two years. Every site we found required re-zoning, and the school district lobbied the city council against re-zoning for each site. Finally, we found a warehouse in an industrial park in Louisville that looked promising. We had nine months to renovate the warehouse and get city approval. We hired teachers subject to the site approval, and we bought all the necessary furnishings and books with a grant we received, but we could not start work on renovating the warehouse until we received the zoning change.

The vote for approval kept being delayed until there was not enough time to renovate. We resigned ourselves to starting the school in the warehouse without renovations. Finally, a few weeks before school was to start, the city voted. We were denied approval. The district's lobbying had stopped us again.

Discouraged, we surrendered. We sent an email to the families that had signed up for our school, explaining that we could not open. The day after sending the email, however, two members of our team were driving through nearby Lafayette when they saw a "For Sale" sign that had just gone up for a day care center. The zoning for a school was already in place, and the building had just the right amount of rooms for our students; there was even a playground and a lunchroom.

The owner agreed to lease the building to us for the first year so that we could move in right away, and we agreed to buy the building a year later. Another email went out to the parents, saying we were going to open after all and asking for volunteers. In a few weeks we had the building scrubbed down, painted, wired for the Internet, and furnished. We opened a week late, but we opened. Today Peak-to-Peak is an ongoing success and is ranked as one the top fifty schools in our nation by both *Newsweek* and *US News & World Report*.

By the end of the '90's, Jerry and I decided we were done with the commercial mortgage business. My marriage also came to an end during that time, and I felt utterly lost. I lived in my office for several months, feeling inadequate when my children visited because I had no home for them. But I learned a valuable lesson. Years later, when I told my son Kenyon how bad I felt that he had to visit me in my office, he surprised me by saying that those were some of his fondest memories. I have related this lesson to many discouraged fathers over the years: just being there is more important to your children than what you are able to give them.

In January of 2000, Jerry and I became two of the co-founders of a startup company. The company developed a novel technology to parallelize software for identifying targets in images, so that computers could spot objects of interest faster than humans. We specialized in finding Russian MIGs in satellite images, but we could identify tumors in medical scans just as easily.

Jerry and I had never financed a startup company before, so we had to learn the art of finding "angels," or individuals willing to invest the money to launch a new company. Learning to do this is especially challenging when you are starting your life over. None of us realized how long and challenging the journey would be.

About a year into the endeavor I received an unusual call. The caller identified himself as a technology scout for the CIA and said he wanted to set up a time to see our computer cluster. I asked when he would like to meet, and he said, "Just open the door when I knock. I'm coming up the stairs right now." That was our introduction to the government.

Over the next few years, we discovered that our approach to parallel processing was world-class, and we met a variety of interesting characters. DARPA, the military's arm for advanced research, helped us with several grants. We were also introduced to the intelligence community and government integrators, as well as Cray, Sun, and IBM.

We became friends with Gene Amdahl, one of the greatest luminaries in high performance computing and the creator of Amdahl's Law. The world owes the architecture of mainframe computers largely to Gene. He was in his senior years when we met him, and he possessed a vast storehouse of knowledge about the early days of computing. He gave us the confidence to forge ahead by vetting some of our CTO's first white papers.

Gene became one of my best friends and a teacher of life lessons. Beyond his achievements and brilliance, he was a man of compassion with great love for his fellow man. I would have lunch with him whenever I visited Silicon Valley. Every time we hit a roadblock, he would encourage me, saying, "That's normal, Scott. That happened to me, too. Keep at it."

My favorite story of his was how he built a house for his wife with his bare hands. He had just returned from WWII and was going to college in South Dakota, but he could find nowhere to live. "There wasn't a single vacancy," he told me. "So I asked the owner of a vacant piece of land for permission to build a rough house, using whatever I could get my hands on, so my wife would be comfortable while I completed school." He added, with a smile, "It was harder to build than I anticipated. I thought I was finished when I was down to the doors. Then I discovered the doors were the hardest part."

Gene's comment sums up every endeavor I have been involved in—they are always harder than you think. And when you think you are almost done, the hardest part has just begun. In fact, there's a saying in software development that software is always "90% done." No doubt Obama can identify with that when he reflects on the development schedule for his healthcare website. The press declared it a debacle due to its tardiness; in my opinion, it was a miracle that it was ever finished at all.

When we first met with the CIA, they said, "We take the most conservative estimate we can wrangle from a development team, and we multiply the time and cost seven-fold. That way, if we're working with seasoned professionals, we'll have an accurate number." Apparently, we weren't the first entrepreneurs to experience unforeseen delays.

When DARPA encouraged us to expand our technology, building a general solution for high performance computing rather than exclusively for image processing, I thought of the CIA's advice. And true to their warning, it was eight years from inception until we finally had a solution nailed down. Even then, we did not receive the traction from the industry we hoped for because we had to parallelize each customer's software ourselves—our methodology proved too complex for others to use.

We brought several industry experts on board to help solve the problem. Tom Gooch, who retired as a senior manager at StorageTek, joined our board of directors, along with John Gustafson, who led Sun's high performance computing project with DARPA. Before Tom joined our company, he read our main white paper. It took him six weeks, and then we met in a coffee shop for him to give me his opinion.

"I have good news and bad news," he said. "Which do you want first?"

"The good news," I said.

"The good news is that your CTO has come up with one of the most brilliant breakthroughs mankind will ever see."

I was elated. What could be bad news after that?

"The bad news is, I have no idea how you're going to make a dime with it," Tom concluded.

My head was reeling. So many years and millions of dollars! "What should we do?" I asked Tom.

"If you can figure out a way to build a development platform for mere mortals, allowing them to write their own software so that it automatically utilizes your algorithms for parallelization, you've got a killer product," Tom said.

It dawned on me that this endeavor would take many more years, and we were already battle-weary. Gene said he thought we could do it. Our CTO said it was impossible. We floundered six more months until we had a breakthrough. That breakthrough allowed us to secure additional funding and bring new expertise into the company. I was able to pass the role of CEO on to John Gustafson, and we hunkered down for several more years of development, which finally led to our current product, Blue Cheetah.

Shortly after John stepped in as CEO, I landed in the hospital with five blood clots in my lungs. I had been feeling awful for some time while flying around the country, but I did not know what was wrong. I thought I could tough it out, but finally, at a conference in Florida, I could go no further. My sister lived nearby, and she insisted on driving me to the emergency room.

The diagnosis was quick, and the doctor voiced his concern to my sister: "If I hadn't seen him so alert, I'd say this was an x-ray of a man who had died of blood clots. I'll give him a ten percent chance of survival because he's so alert."

I had a strange experience while in the hospital. I felt a cold, dark presence come into the room and settle next to me. It remained all night. Eventually it dawned on me that this could be what people referred to as the "spirit of death."

It was popular, at the time, to assert that man could manifest his own destiny if he exerted his will. As I sensed the immense power of the presence next to me, I thought of that idea and laughed. "They never met this thing," I concluded. The idea that the will of man could have any power over what I was sensing seemed humorous.

As I lay there, contemplating the presence beside me, I felt no fear. It seemed to me that the hand of God was holding back the presence that had come for me, and that I would be fine. The reality of my mortality, however, took on a new meaning for me because of the experience, and to this day that has never changed. Up until then, my mortality had been an abstract concept—today my mortality seems very real to me. And as odd as it sounds, I have no fear of death anymore.

The clots in my lungs forced me to surrender, relinquishing control of the company's progress. And once again, it was the best thing I could have done. As I lay in the hospital, I received text messages because I could not talk on the phone, and one by one, everything on my "to do" list was accomplished. When I was released from the hospital a week later, Blue Cheetah was ready to forge ahead with a world-class team in place. I was able to take time off to recover.

During my recovery process, I learned a powerful lesson. A friend called shortly after I left the hospital and asked whether I thought there could be a spiritual root to my condition. The clots were still in my lungs at the time, since they take a couple of months to be absorbed by the body, so I could feel their pain and was unable to take deep breaths.

I told my friend that I did feel there was a connection to an issue I had been battling for months. I felt like I needed to do more about the situation, to step up and fight, but I was stymied. There were too many terrible ramifications involved. My friend suggested I call a counselor at Dr. Henry Wright's church in Georgia. I knew of Dr. Wright's work in linking the roots of various diseases to chronic fear, worry, bitterness, anger, and so forth, so I agreed.

I called expecting the counselor to galvanize me, to say I needed to overcome fear and take action no matter the consequences. So instead of telling him my situation, I tested him. I asked him if Dr. Wright's mission had any experience with blood clots in the lungs. He said they had seen a few cases, and so far it had been the same in every case; each person suffered from deep bitterness and anger, with intent to retaliate. The solution was not to take action as I had been thinking, but to forgive and surrender the problem to the Lord.

I was surprised at how defensive I became. I protested, "You don't understand what's involved. This is serious!"

He replied, "It is serious. It's killing you."

What he said sank in. I ended up praying earnestly, forgiving and asking forgiveness. I was sincere. I kept thinking of the dark spirit that had come for me. I was being given a second chance.

Almost immediately, I felt different. I could breathe deeply, and there was no more pain. As it turns out, I had to learn the lesson twice more. A week later I found myself riled up again, thinking I needed to do something. Within hours the same sickening pain returned to my chest, and my lungs tightened up. When I let go of the anger, the pain went away. I had the same experience a week later, except this time I thanked God for the lesson, acknowledging the barometer he had put in my chest.

On my way back to Colorado, I stopped to visit my doctor in Florida, and he insisted on taking me around his office. "See, this is the patient I was telling you about!" he said excitedly, as he showed me to his colleagues. "He checked in with five clots in his lungs, and now look at him; he's as strong as an ox!" I have been fine ever since.

Today Blue Cheetah is finally productized, a platform that ports legacy software to the cloud. For decades the software that runs our nation's Fortune 500 companies has been written for mainframe computers. But today, cloud computing is the way to go. All the old software needs to be rewritten to run on the cloud. It's an enormous task, and our platform automates the process, while also modernizing a company's software.

Kidz Magazine also evolved. Several years ago we faced a crisis because Google drove the price of advertising so low that it was no longer feasible to publish. We decided to move the magazine online to cut distribution costs, but we needed an innovative format to keep the attention of our student audience. Simply publishing the students' work online would not hold their interest, so we decided to build a platform that would allow students to create their own video games and social media apps.

In order to accomplish this, we pulled together a team of entrepreneurs in Boulder. My son Matthew led the team, and two years into the project they had a compelling prototype. When I saw how easy it was to create apps on the platform they had designed, it occurred to me that the product was not just for children anymore. I was not sure, however, how to tell the team that I thought we should repurpose the company.

As it turned out, the team was ahead of me, and they were hoping I would see it that way, too. We adopted the product name Fathym, and we began building a platform that would allow non-developers to easily create sophisticated apps. Fathym also connects logic and data in a unique way, making it a powerful solution for the rapidly emerging Internet of Things. Right now, data is kept in silos, accessible only by the app specifically designed to process the data. If the user of the app wants to do something with the data other than what the app is hardwired to do, a programmer must rewrite the app.

Fathym solves this problem. It allows the user to modify an app, and it allows other users to create apps accessing the same data for their own purposes. With Fathym, for example, you could have an Excel spreadsheet running inside a Word document. And you could repurpose Excel or Word as you see fit.

In addition to my involvement with Blue Cheetah and Fathym, I returned to structured finance and filed a series of patents. I developed a number of financial structures to improve the return on investments made in private equity funds. As the filings advanced, we formed a fund based upon the patent portfolio that I had developed. That fund continues to grow, and today it is a major investor in both Blue Cheetah and Fathym.

While it is gratifying to see these companies grow, the lessons I have learned from the many challenges they presented are far more important. I have come to believe that the saying "No pain, no gain" applies to all of life, not just the gym.

The process of learning through hardship is often a surprising one. In order to love and experience peace, for instance, we must learn to forgive. And in order to forgive, we must be wronged. This principle provides a powerful context for understanding the ups and downs in life.

In order to navigate the unfairness of life, we must let go of bitterness, judgment, covetousness, and anger. We must learn to forgive. In order to do this, however, we must experience that which provokes bitterness, judgment, and so forth—we must be wronged. There is no other way to learn such lessons. Life, it seems, is unfair for our own good, a profound truth worth taking to heart.

For most of my life, I was either an atheist or an agnostic. Today, I have a deep faith in God. And as with many, my faith was born from being pushed to the limit. I had racked up many mistakes, my marriage had ended, and I was in the midst of far longer and more arduous journeys than I had ever imagined with Blue Cheetah and Fathym.

My crisis caused me to go back and review what I had studied in college—Jungian psychology, Buddhism, philosophy, and so forth. I read *Siddhartha* again, and I longed for the peace by the river that Siddhartha experienced toward the end of his life.

I also read *The Four Agreements*, a text of ancient Toltec wisdom. It is a good book, and I recommend it. But something was missing. My business partner Jerry recommended I read the Bible, which I did, but I did not like what I read. There is a passage in the Bible that says if you do not already have faith, the scriptures will appear objectionable, and from my experience that is truc.

Finally, after a year of concerted effort, I met with Jerry and said it was no use. I could never have blind faith, as I was too honest with myself. I would always know I had decided to believe something with no real basis.

Jerry replied, "Of course you cannot have blind faith. That *would* be meaningless. What you just said makes total sense." Then he asked, "Do you know what the Bible says about faith? It says that faith is by the grace of God. God has to give you faith. You can't just decide that God exists on your own."

"Well, that's even more unfair," I said. "If there is a God, and he has kept his existence from me, what's that all about?"

"I don't know," Jerry answered. "Perhaps God wants you to ask him instead of trying to figure it out yourself."

He went on to say that he had gone on a similar journey. His life had spiraled until he could continue no further, and he had finally appealed to God for help.

He concluded, "Scott, if you ask God for the truth sincerely, from your heart, and nothing happens, then I am wrong."

That night, back at home, I thought about it and concluded that I could not do such a thing. I had no basis to do so. In fact, it seemed silly. Then something in me stirred, and I thought to myself, "Now the thumbscrews will be tightened." And I was right.

For years I had raised money successfully, but from that point on I could no longer raise a dime. The possible connection between my inability to raise money and my avoidance of God was not lost on me, but asking still seemed a foolish thing to do. I held fast, and the company's reserves dwindled.

This went on for months, until we were down to our final payroll. I flew to California for some last-ditch meetings, and during the flight the plane hit severe turbulence. I watched as people gripped their armrests, thinking, "How irrational people are! At 500 mph, you can't hold yourself in your seat if the plane crashes."

The turbulence increased, and soon I felt the urge to grip my own seat, but I resisted. "I don't want to be a fool," I said to myself.

Then I pictured the plane plowing into the mountains. Just as it was about to crash, I imagined all the people waving their arms and screaming, "God help us!" In my fantasy, I remained calm, logically waiting to see what would happen.

As I imagined the plane crashing, a thought intruded: "Who's the fool? At least they are asking for help!"

The connection was not lost on me. Our company was about to crash, and I was too stubborn to ask God if he existed. "I would leave no stone unturned to help the company," I thought. "Why would I not ask?"

As the plane neared San Jose, I thought it over. Was I avoiding prayer because it would be embarrassing to say I believed in God? I acknowledged that pride was a factor, but not the limiting factor. I also considered whether I was afraid of any changes I would have to make in my life. Again, fear was a factor, but I thought I could handle the changes.

It dawned on me that, deep down, I felt like it was all for naught. I was sure God was fictitious, and I was certain to be disappointed. I felt enormous resistance to the whole idea. Really, I was quite stubborn.

Then I asked myself a logical "If, then" question: "*If* there were a God, *would* I want to know?" I realized it was a very good question. I could see someone deciding they would rather not know, and for quite a few reasons. In my case, however, I decided I would want to know. In fact, I would be quite curious.

Next I asked myself, "*If* there were a God, *would* I want to follow his will?" Again, it was a good question, as I could see someone observing the nature of the world and deciding they would rather have nothing to do with God. In my case, I determined that I would want to follow God. In fact, it would be important to me.

Those two questions were the key for me, and answering them is within our logical domain. *We have the basis to make those choices.* Once I had consciously made those choices, I could ask with sincerity. It still seemed to me that God did not exist, but I was now comfortable asking because I had decided where I stood if God did exist.

So, what happened when I asked? The truth is that, for you, it should not matter. You cannot rely on my story to arrive at an answer for such a question. If you base your faith on me, you will eventually be disappointed. What matters is what happens for *you* if you decide to ask. If I am right, your faith must come by the grace of God and not by the word of man.

If you ask God for the truth sincerely, from your heart, and nothing happens, then perhaps I am wrong. You may have to ask more than once, and you may have to wait. You may even have to search your heart for sincerity and settle for yourself whether you would be willing to follow God if he is real. But based on my experience, he will eventually make himself known to you.

When I asked, I was brutally honest. I prayed, "I would like to know if you are real, and if you are, I would like to follow you." But I also told God that I doubted he was real, admitting that I felt like a desperate man grasping for straws. I added that I felt certain I would be disappointed in the end.

My investor meeting the next morning was a dud. As I drove back to the hotel, however, I received a call from an investor I had pitched many months ago. He said, "This morning I was thinking about Blue Cheetah, and I thought, 'Why didn't I invest?' So I'm calling to ask you if the opportunity is still open."

I told him it was, and he said he would send a check that day. A little later, he told me that his brother wanted to invest and would also send a check that day. A few minutes after that, he called me again; he had just remembered meeting someone at a party who had expressed an interest in investing. He gave me their number.

I called the gentleman, and he was happy to hear from me. When I asked if he had time to hear about the investment, he said, "I really don't have time right now. What I need are the wiring instructions. I'll wire the funds today, and you can tell me all about it some other time."

I had enough experience in raising money to know that such things do not normally happen. With the news of the first two investments, I quickly prayed, "Lord, this doesn't constitute proof, but if you did this, I can't thank you enough. I reaffirm that I want to know if you are real, and if you are real, I want to follow you."

With the promise of the third check, I prayed, "Look, this could go on all day, and it wouldn't constitute proof. But if you did this, thank you. I repeat that I want to know the truth about you, and if you are real, I want to follow you."

Back at the hotel, I called Jerry, who was writing dismissal letters for our employees. I realized I had a choice about which subject to tell him first—the news about the money, or the news that I had prayed. I decided to tell him about praying because I knew he cared deeply about the subject, and he wept at the news.

When he had composed himself, he said, "Scott, this is an answer to my prayers. Last night, I was praying about Blue Cheetah's finances when I suddenly knew I had to answer a question before the Lord. 'Jerry, which is more important: Scott's salvation, or the survival of the company?' Of course I said, 'Why Lord, it would be Scott's salvation.' Then I was at peace, and I slept like a baby for the first time in months."

I said, "Jerry, I'm touched, but you don't have to worry about the company!"

I told him about the money coming in. With the story of each check he exclaimed, "Why Scott, that's a miracle!" And I replied, "Well, I'll allow that it may be. It is unusual."

Nothing else happened for months, and then one day I felt different. God seemed real to me. It was that simple. I had faith, which has grown immensely over the years and is now an integral part of my ability to love and experience peace.

Today I attend church and read the Bible. I pray and find answers in prayer. In years past, I would never have imagined that to be my life. When I look back, I am humbled by how many mistakes I have made, just as I am humbled by the number of mistakes I continue to make. Today I have a clear understanding of the lyrics to the song "Amazing Grace."

Just as we must learn to forgive in order to love, I believe we are forgiven because we are loved. It is a measure of the depth of God's love for us. The truth is a beautiful thing, and it is indeed worth asking for.

It is because of my faith that I am pursuing public office to implement the changes proposed in this book. Otherwise, I would never consider such an undertaking. Politically speaking, I am nobody, but I feel compelled to help establish the dawning of a New American Dream. How it will unfold is in the hands of God.

CHAPTER NINE

OUR JOURNEY
The Road Home

BECAUSE WE ARE running our nation on an outdated operating system, we are limiting the capacity of our economy. The financial solutions I advocate solve this problem. Our nation's journey, however, is about more than just money.

A supporter of mine once told me he thought I was the economic savior for our nation. I told him to think of me as the nation's plumber. We have a cash flow problem, and I am here to fix the pipes so the money flows better.

Another supporter, a self-proclaimed anarchist, had a different view. He said I was the first politician who did not make him want to throw up when I mentioned God. The truth is, while it is of vital importance to update our economic system, I believe the spiritual aspects of our nation are even more important. A thriving nation is not simply a prosperous one, but one whose citizens choose kindness over criticism and gratitude over greed.

In the previous chapter, I mentioned that I traveled around the world in an airstream trailer as a child. What impressed me the most about the trip was how we were greeted as Americans. We were heroes everywhere we went. In Iran, the locals whisked us off to visit a dam that the Americans had built. In Afghanistan, a family invited us to their tent to drink tea. It saddens me to think of how our nation is regarded today. To a large measure we have squandered our legacy.

I think one reason for the change in sentiment toward our nation can be found in Oswald Chambers book *My Utmost For His Highest*.[48] Chambers quotes one of Jesus' most sobering statements, recorded in Matthew 7:1: "Judge not, that you be not judged" (*New King James Version*). Then Chambers expands:

> Jesus' instructions with regard to judging others is very simply put; He says, "Don't." The average Christian is the most piercingly critical individual known. Criticism is one of the ordinary activities of people, but in the spiritual realm nothing is accomplished by it. . . . The Holy Spirit is the only one in the proper position to criticize, and He alone is able to show what is wrong without hurting and wounding. It is impossible to enter into fellowship with God when you are in a critical

---

[48] James Reimann, *My Utmost For His Highest*, Discovery House, 1992

mood. Criticism serves to make you harsh, vindictive, and cruel, and leaves you with the soothing and flattering idea that you are somehow superior to others. . . .

If I see the little speck in your eye, it means that I have a plank of timber in my own (see 7:3–5). Every wrong thing that I see in you, God finds in me. Every time I judge, I condemn myself (see Romans 2:17–24). Stop having a measuring stick for other people. There is always at least one more fact, which we know nothing about, in every person's situation. . . . I have never met a person I could despair of, or lose all hope for, after discerning what lies in me apart from the grace of God. (575 – 577)

When I first read this passage it deeply moved me. I realized it addressed a theme I had not yet introduced in my book—how to come together as a nation. Then the following email rolled in as a daily devotional from Richard Rohr:[49]

If we begin by distinguishing between the "holy people" and the "unholy people," we end up with what we have now, which is largely an exclusionary religion. We don't have a strong passion about what we are *for*,

---

[49] cac.org

but we just know what we are *against*, what is wrong, what we must not do, and who is sinful.

Reading Rohr's email, I realized this same theme applies to our nation. When we start criticizing one another, we cease to be a light to the world. Instead, we become a laughing stock—and we lose our influence.

Today we are a divided nation and very critical of each other. The news is full of venomous judgment. I believe criticism is keeping us from achieving the unity we need to be a truly thriving nation.

Many Christians are up in arms about the moral condition of our nation. Ironically, much of the criticism of the West by Muslims is about the same thing. When we look about us, whether we are an adherent to any particular faith or not, the world can seem a moral mess. Our initial instinct is to find someone to blame, and so we find conservatives blaming liberals, Democrats blaming Republicans, and religious people blaming non-religious people. Instead of blaming each other for the mess, we need to ask ourselves, "In light of all that is going on, how can we work together to improve our situation?"

I think the answer to this question can be found in Chambers' words: "Stop having a measuring stick for other people" (577). This makes sense if we believe that only God is capable of right judgment—that only he is able to show us what is wrong in our lives without hurting us. If we truly believe in the absolute sovereignty of God—that he does, in fact, have things in full control—then we really *can* leave judgment to him and learn to love one another.

Oswald Chambers finds a purpose to the mess that we perceive when he writes: "Every wrong thing that I see in you, God finds in me. Every time I judge, I condemn myself" (576). In other words, God teaches us to improve by giving us the world as our mirror. Rabbi Israel Baal Shem Tov expressed it this way: "Should you look upon your fellow man and see a blemish, it is your own imperfection that you are encountering—you are being shown what it is that you must correct within yourself."[50]

The scriptures are counterintuitive. Instead of taking charge, they advise us to trust God. Instead of judgment, they advise forgiveness. And instead of despair when things do not go our way, they advise praise. Praising God when things are in disarray is not our natural response.

I finally understood the power of praise in the face of difficulty when I read Merlin Carothers' book *Prison to Praise*.[51] Carothers states that when we learn to praise God in *all* things, we come to grasp that God is in control. He writes:

---

[50] www.azquotes.com/author/19657-Baal_Shem_Tov

[51] Merlin Carothers, *Prison to Praise*, Logos International, 1970

In Luke 6:23 Jesus tells us that we are to leap for joy. He even describes when we are to leap for joy: "When you are hungry. . . when men shall hate you. . . when men shall reproach you. . . when they cast out your name as evil. . . rejoice in that day and leap for joy." (69)

Carothers had a hard time believing this at first, confessing, "Infirmities were the very things. . . . I had not been enjoying. I didn't like it when people turned against me; I didn't like it when accidents happened and things went wrong" (69). Once convicted that God was in charge of everything, however, Carothers learned to praise God for all things, and he began to see his troubles as gifts.

Carothers writes, "Satan can't do a thing to us unless he first gets God's permission" (76). In other words, no bad situation takes God by surprise. If he allows suffering in our lives, he must have a reason for it. This is a staggering concept. It is not one that we can easily wrap our hearts around.

Carothers applied this lesson to his life with remarkable results, and after reading his book I began to do the same. Today I am convinced that God is not wringing his hands over the state of the world. Instead, I believe he has purposefully given us the challenges that are in front of us to help us grow. That includes racial tensions, our financial problems, and even ISIS.

If we seek to solve our challenges with the confidence that God is in charge, we will see our problems in a new light. Chambers writes, "It is impossible to enter into fellowship with God when you are in a critical mood" (576). In the same way, it is impossible to enter into fellowship with each other to solve problems when we are in a critical mood. The scriptures say that if you love God, you will love your fellow man. And if you love your fellow man, you will find it easier to work through problems.

There is an old adage that skips the spiritual banter and sums up the situation pragmatically: "You attract more flies with honey than you do with vinegar." This underscores why we are better at solving problems when we speak kindly than when we lambast one another. It also explains why we do more for world peace when we conduct business with our neighbors than when we invade them.

The financial solutions herein are predicated upon win-win relationships. Not only could they serve to improve our nation's economy, they could strengthen our leadership in world affairs. Currently the contributions that our nation makes to the World Bank and the IMF tax our economy. Under Banking 2.0, however, we could dramatically increase our role in capitalizing growth around the world, but instead of draining our economy, we could profit.

There is one final thought that I would like to share with you. While I am optimistic about our future, my optimism stems from my faith in God's plan as outlined in the scriptures. I am not naïve about human nature.

Because of technology, we enjoy many luxuries today that even the wealthiest of kings did not posses a century ago: air travel, cell phones, and the Internet, to name a few. If it were not for human nature, the financial solutions proposed in this book, combined with today's technology, would give us the means to create a utopia. The trouble with too much material wealth, however, is that it makes people greedy.

I believe the prosperity that we could realize from the solutions in this book would affect us the same way manna affected the Jews in their march through the desert (see Numbers ch. 11, Exodus ch. 16). Every morning God sent bread for the Jews to eat. For the first time, they did not have to labor for their food. As soon as they grew accustomed to God's providence, though, they began to grumble and demand meat. So God sent flocks of quail—and they ate until they were violently ill (Num. 11:33).

As our prosperity grows, if someday you sense that a time has come when we are overcome with greed, and you feel that we are building a new Babylon instead of a sound America, do not despair. Instead, keep your faith that God is in charge. Indeed, praise him for such times, for they too are a part his plan. Remember, that what many will despair as being the "end times" will actually herald our salvation, which, it is written, shall come as a thief in the night.

Acknowledgements

I WOULD LIKE to thank my grandfathers for showing me that being in business and doing right by your fellow man are not mutually exclusive. My Grandfather Cordes would meet with newly hired employees to help them create a budget. He loved his employees, just as he loved his customers, and his unwavering goal was to provide the best for everyone. This is the grandfather who gave me a bearer bond, which led to the idea of Coupon Stripping.

My Grandfather Smith was the CEO of a public utility. He took pride in the fact that he never raised prices during his decades at the helm. He delighted in climbing power poles to help out when there was a power outage, startling more than one lineman when they recognized the CEO working alongside them.

When grandfather took over the company, it was at the end of a long battle with regulators, which resulted in the company having to return money to its customers. His first act as CEO was to set up tables in the city park and invite customers to receive an immediate refund. "Give them their money with a *smile*," he insisted. "This is the opportunity to mend our relationship with our customers!"

The attitude my grandfathers had toward business guided me in formulating my solutions for the economy. Economics is about providing for everyone. It is about win-win solutions. It is about caring for our fellow man.

Thank you to Stephen Shepherd for drawing the connections between my abstract economic concepts and their direct effects on our personal lives. Stephen helped define the heart and soul of my proposals. His deep understanding of my proposal has been vital in keeping the project true to its course.

I am also grateful to my wife, Sheri, for her extensive editing. Like Stephen, she saw the need to touch people's hearts rather than present dry economic solutions. The final book bears little resemblance to my first draft, and Sheri made more changes than anyone else. She wrote some of the copy herself, careening sections hither and thither and tossing out everything that was too tedious.

I am very grateful to Marie Campbell, my content editor, for picking up where Sheri left off. She re-organized the book and simplified my economic descriptions so that they are finally understandable. Skye Kerr did a wonderful job as my copy editor, and it is amazing to me how someone can be so fast and so accurate at the same time.

Working with illustrator Steve Hussey to create the cartoons and diagrams in this book was pure joy. A picture is worth a thousand words, but Steve's pictures are worth much more—they bring my dry economic concepts to life. It was Sheri's mom, Debbie Burnham, who suggested the use of art and characters.

Many thanks to Cybelle Lyon for her encouragement, copy edits, and advice; Rick Bennett for his help in framing and positioning; Curt Pessman for his help in the early stages of this book; Carrie Momeni for her ruthless pursuit of clarity; Stuart Cohen for his extensive analysis and comments; Jane Salzman for her enthusiasm and support of this project; Randi Kalish for her suggestions on how to improve the presentation; David Kalish for his critical analysis and strategic advice; Len Brooks for his financial analysis and comments; Rachel Thor for teaching me shortcuts on my Apple; Richard Madison for his daring rescues; Sloan Beatty for his inspiring story; and my business partners

Jerry Verbeck, Rick Thabet, and Shannon Kendall for keeping the lights on.

I would also like to give special thanks to Mickey Lohr, John Lee, and Vince Jordan for their scriptural advice and prayers.

Finally, I would like to thank my family and children for their love, support, and encouragement over the years. They provided the foundation that made this book possible.

ABOUT THE AUTHOR

WITH A BACKGROUND in Wall Street finance, Scott Smith is a serial entrepreneur, having co-founded companies in such diverse industries as agriculture, finance, educational media, and technology. He began his career as a pioneer grower of Sunburst tangerines, helping to develop a market for the fruit and establish the variety's popularity in North America.

In the 1990s, Scott was an early pioneer in structured finance, developing the model for conduit financing. On the strength of his idea, his firm secured a one-billion-dollar line of credit from the investment bank Donaldson, Lufkin & Jenrette in 1993. His model was rapidly adopted by Wall Street and used for securitizing many forms of debt. Later that decade, Scott formed a firm to structure the financing for President Nelson Mandela's Redevelopment Program, which helped provide affordable housing for some 11,000 families near Soweto.

Scott founded Kidz Magazine in 1995, which was one of the earliest examples of user-generated content. As its circulation spanned 30 nations, readership soared into the millions. During this period Scott also served as co-founder and board member of two nationally-ranked charter schools in Colorado: Summit Middle School and Peak-to-Peak K–12.

In the past decade, Scott helped co-found four enterprises: C Squared, FinaTech, Blue Cheetah, and Fathym. C Squared is an angel fund employing a patent-pending financial structure. FinaTech is a developer of a patent portfolio of financial structures that increases the yield on investments in private equity funds. Blue Cheetah is a solution for porting legacy software applications to the cloud, and Fathym provides a platform for creating social media applications.

Scott lives in Boulder, Colorado with his wife, Sheri, founder of the Indigo Education Company. He has six children and enjoys painting galaxies in his spare time.

Made in the USA
Middletown, DE
27 July 2015